REC'D SEP 0 7 2019

FEVER YEAR

The Killer Flu of 1918

A Tragedy in Three Acts

WRITTEN AND
ILLUSTRATED BY
DON BROWN

HOUGHTON MIFFLIN HARCOURT
Boston   New York

Dedicated to the Centers for Disease Control and Prevention,
an underappreciated American treasure.

hmhbooks.com

The illustrations in this book are pen & ink with digital paint.
The text type was set in Appareo.
The display type was set in Chase.

ISBN: 978-0-544-83740-9

Manufactured in China
SCP 10 9 8 7 6 5 4 3 2 1
4500761161

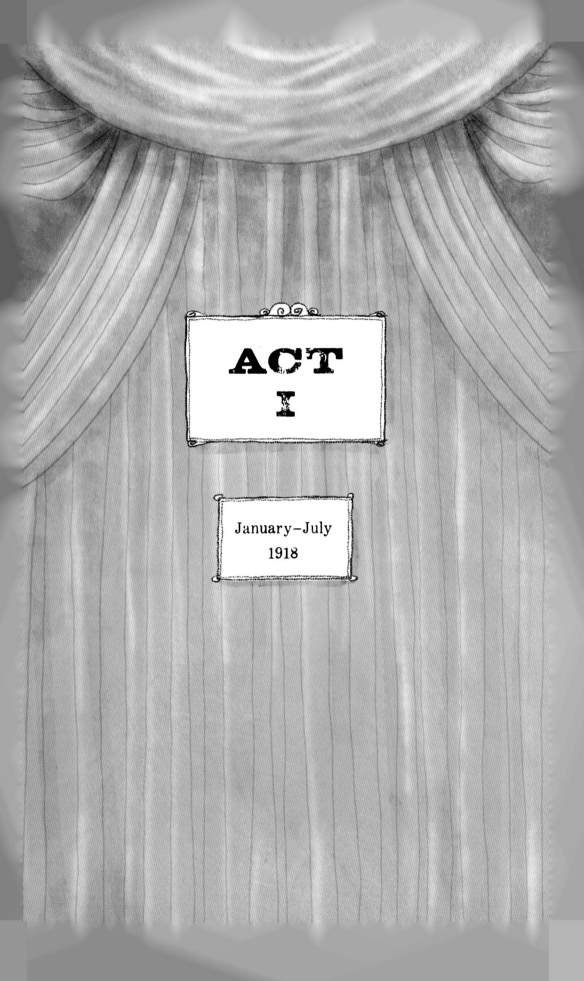

ACT I

January–July 1918

New Year's Day, 1918.

America was at war.

Instead of thousands of joyous, riotous New Year's celebrators, New York City's Times Square was empty. People had decided to ration happiness along with beef and chicken.

Americans were certain of victory. But they had no idea that the world was on the threshold of a ruthless fevered year that would bring sickness to a third of the planet and death to millions of people.

And even if they had known, there was almost nothing they could have done to stop it.

Europe had been at war since 1914. America had mostly sided against Germany. Germany responded by using submarines to sink American ships carrying people and goods to German enemies England and France. Anger against German behavior led to an American declaration of war against Germany in April 1917.

Millions of American citizens joined the fight. Hundreds of thousands of new recruits shuffled here and there around the United States to train for European battlefields. Nicknamed "doughboys," they carried with them patriotism, certainty of victory, hope for a safe return, and . . . disease.

Infectious disease has accompanied armies for all time. Of the Civil War's dead, two out of three were killed by disease.

In March 1918, an army cook Albert Gitchell reported sick to Camp Funston. He was one of roughly 56,000 recruits housed in the Kansas camp.

Soon, more soldiers made their way to the camp hospital, all complaining of fever, sore throat, and headache.

More than a thousand fell ill over the next month. Forty-eight died.

Dr. Loring Miner of Haskell County, less than three hundred miles from Camp Funston, wouldn't have been surprised. Prior to the sickness at Camp Funston, Dr. Miner had helped his patients battle an illness of unusual violence.

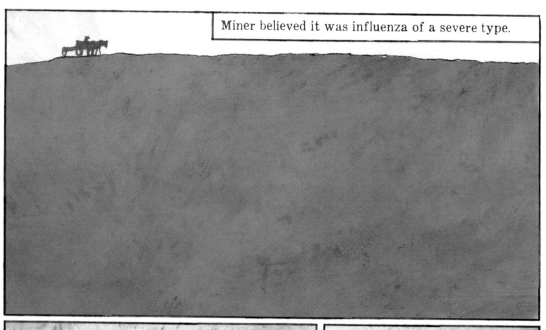

Miner believed it was influenza of a severe type.

It seemed to strike the most fit and healthy, an odd turn for a disease that numbered the youngest and oldest as its most likely victims.

During the outbreak, local Haskell County boys—now army recruits—made trips between Camp Funston and home. As the disease was ending in Haskell County, army cook Gitchell fell ill.

Were the soldiers of Camp Funston victims of the Haskell County outbreak?

After the outbreak at Camp Funston, army camps around the country reported influenza. Then, in Detroit, a thousand Ford Motor Company workers fell ill.

In California, influenza struck about five hundred inmates at San Quentin Prison.

By April, flu struck an American camp near Bordeaux, France, a chief entry place for newly arriving doughboys. Soon British and French soldiers fell victim. The flu leaped the no-man's-land separating the opposing forces and struck the German Army.

Within four months of its appearance in the United States, people all over the globe fell ill to influenza. Its appearance in Spain was openly reported; Spain played no part in the war, so there was no reason to censor critical health news from enemies. People everywhere mistakenly drew a line between Spain and the flu's beginnings, calling it the "Spanish" influenza, much to Spain's displeasure. The name stuck.

SPANISH FLU!

Whatever it was called, influenza was no stranger to anyone.

Some believe the Greeks endured flu—a feverish disease that attacks breathing—as early as 430 CE. There is evidence of an 1173 epidemic in England, Germany, and France.

FOR IT BEGAN . . . WITH A PAIN IN THE HEAD, BACK, AND SOME OF THE LIMBS. . . . THERE WAS FEVER, VIOLENT COUGHS, PAIN IN THE SIDES, AND DIFFICULTY BREATHING.

More epidemics followed. The Italians believed the disease was the work of the the heavens—the moon and the stars.

Ex influential colesti, they said, meaning the sick were under a celestial influence.

Eventually, the disease simply became known as *una influenza.*

The flu could afflict people across great swatches of the globe in events known as pandemics. In 1889, a flu pandemic started in Russia, burned through Europe, leaped to North America, then spread to Latin America and Asia.

Although ninety-nine out of a hundred victims recovered from the Russian flu, the death toll still reached a million people.

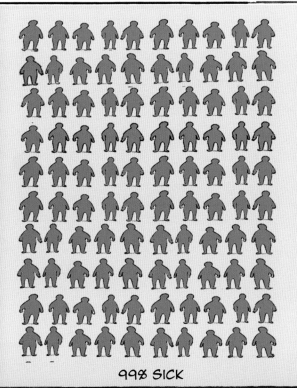

1% DIED =
1 MILLION DEAD

99% SICK

By 1918, most people thought of the flu as merely an annoyance. Yes, it threatened the very young and the very old, but science and medicine were defeating disease and the flu's days were surely numbered. . . . But they were wrong.

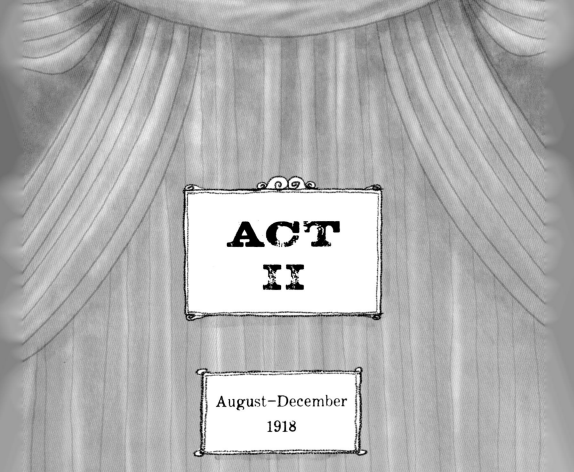

ACT II

August–December
1918

On August 15, 1918, an English warship arrived in Freetown, Sierra Leone, with hundreds of sick sailors aboard.

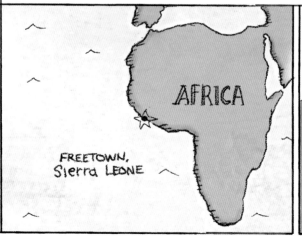

They suffered chills and crushing headaches. Their muscles ached. They burned with fever. They coughed and coughed and coughed.

After loading the ship with coal, hundreds of African laborers fell sick with similar ailments.

Soon after, another British warship steamed into Sierra Leone. She sailed away with fuel and disease. Six hundred of her 779-man crew fell ill. Fifty-one died.

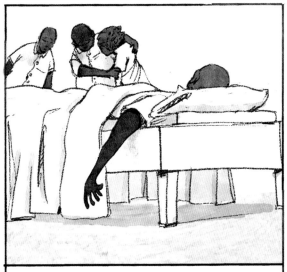

In Sierra Leone, the illness spread and killed more than a thousand Africans.

About a week later, on August 27, three sailors at the Commonwealth Pier in Boston, Massachusetts, became sick.

On Wednesday, there were **8** cases. On Thursday, 58. Then **81**, followed by 106.

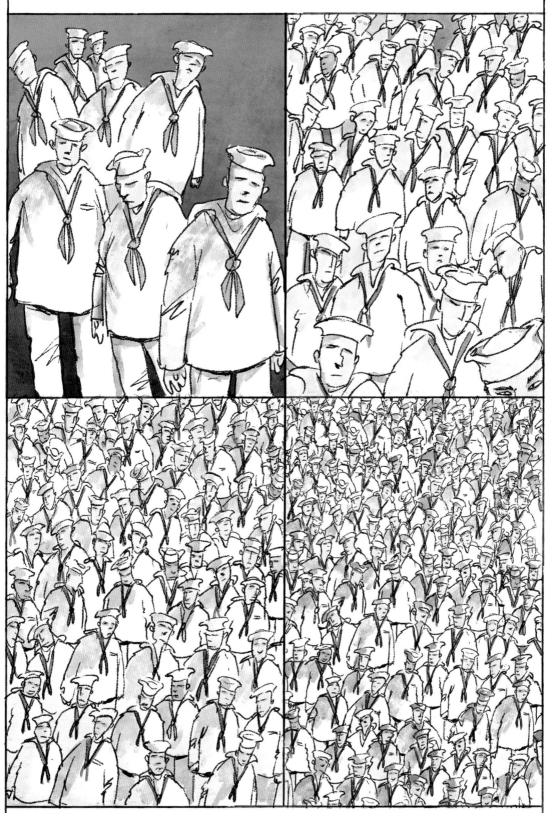

The unluckiest developed pneumonia—a disease of the lungs—and more than half of those sufferers died.

Thirty-five miles northwest of the pier, 45,000 soldiers crowded the Camp Devens army base. On September 7, 1918, an infantryman reported sick.

The infection exploded; the hospital overflowed with eight thousand patients. In one twenty-four-hour period, sixty-six men died.

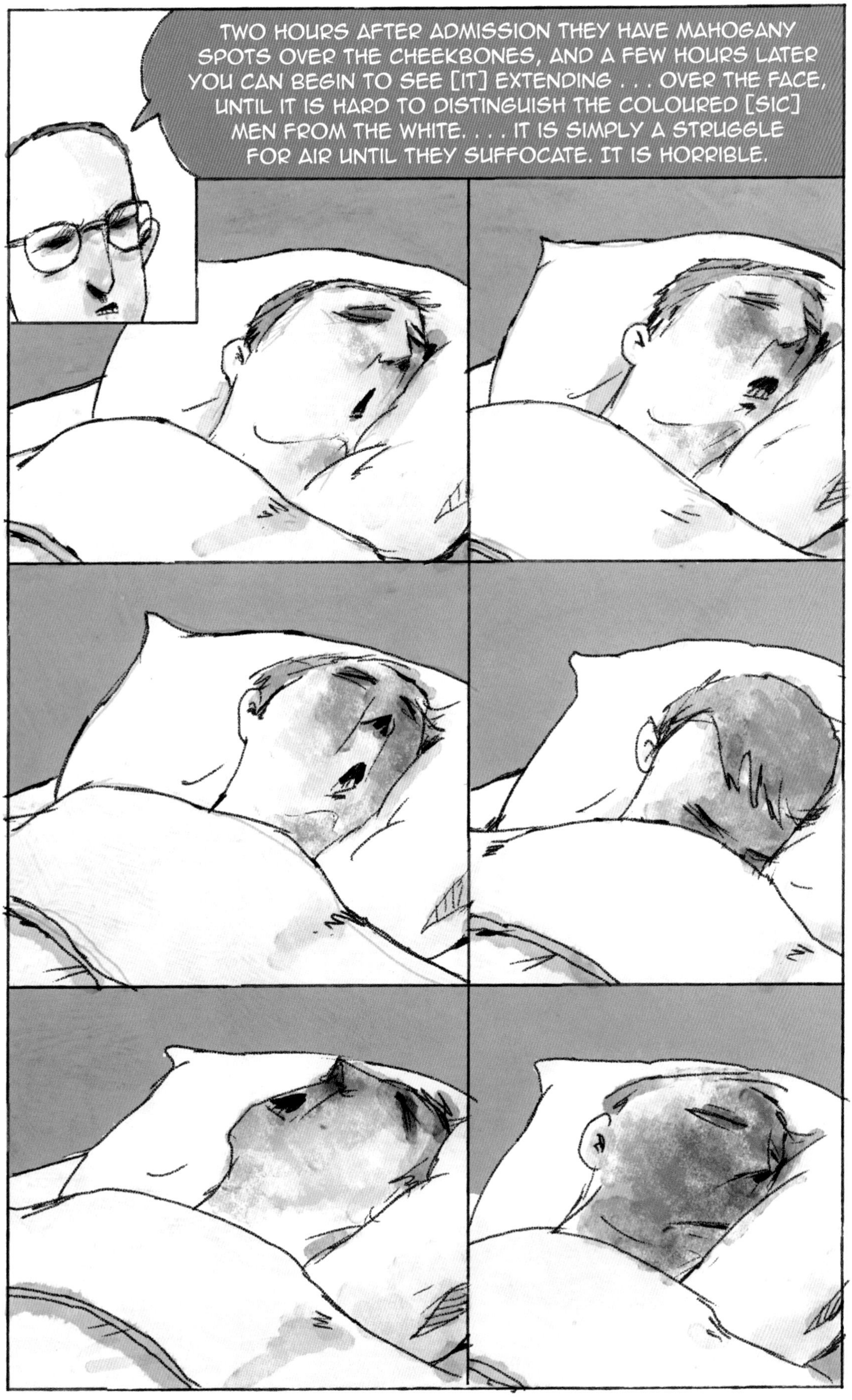
TWO HOURS AFTER ADMISSION THEY HAVE MAHOGANY SPOTS OVER THE CHEEKBONES, AND A FEW HOURS LATER YOU CAN BEGIN TO SEE [IT] EXTENDING . . . OVER THE FACE, UNTIL IT IS HARD TO DISTINGUISH THE COLOURED [SIC] MEN FROM THE WHITE. . . . IT IS SIMPLY A STRUGGLE FOR AIR UNTIL THEY SUFFOCATE. IT IS HORRIBLE.

The army dispatched Dr. William Welch to Camp Devens. Welch stood at the forefront of American medicine. Accompanying the good doctor were other renowned physicians.

They were met by hundreds of young soldiers, in groups of ten and more, trudging to the base hospital, blankets in hand and coughing blood in spasmodic fits.

Some collapsed in the rain.

Without enough nurses, the sick climbed into cots on their own.

Beds spilled out of the wards and on to porches.

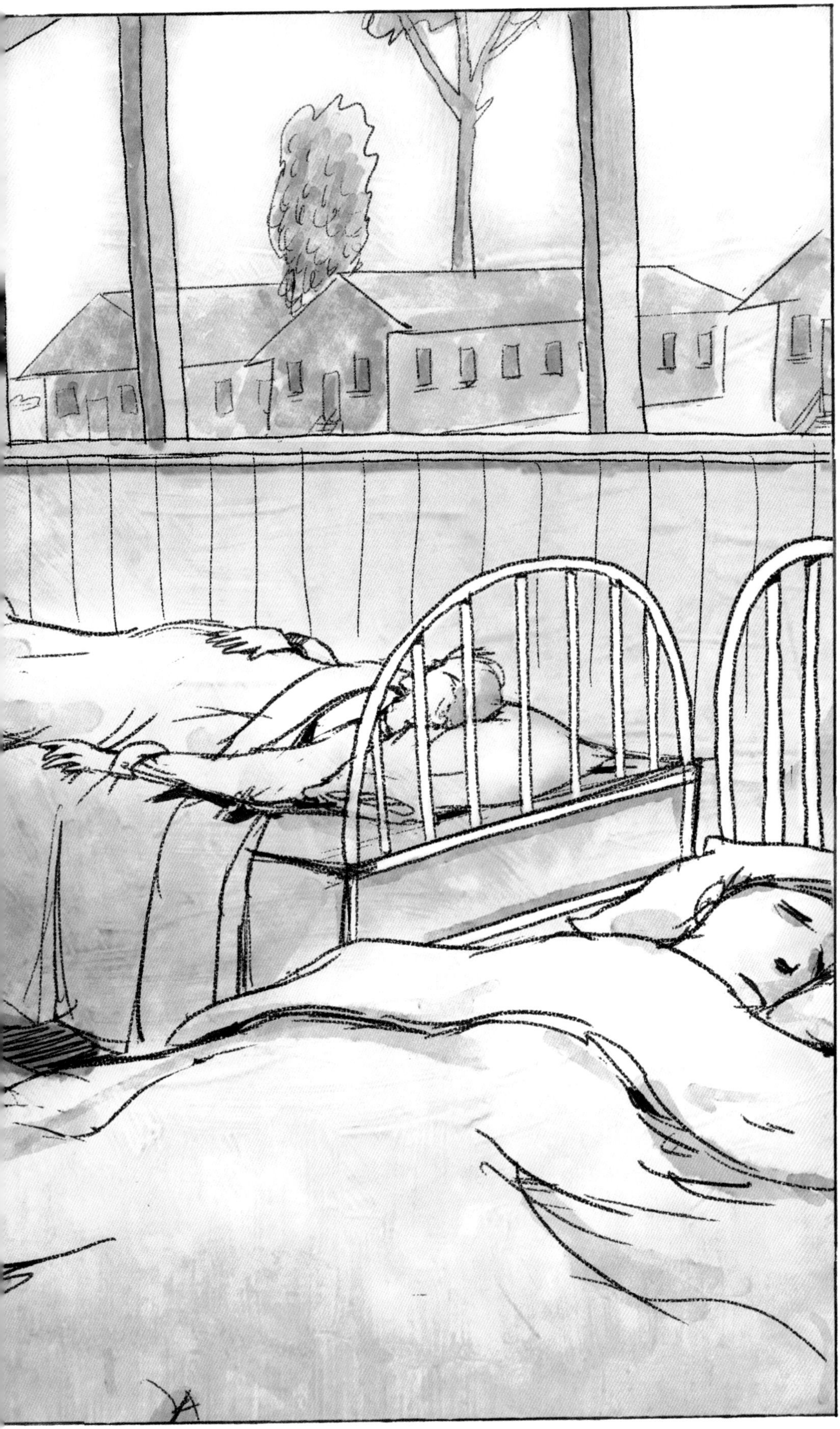

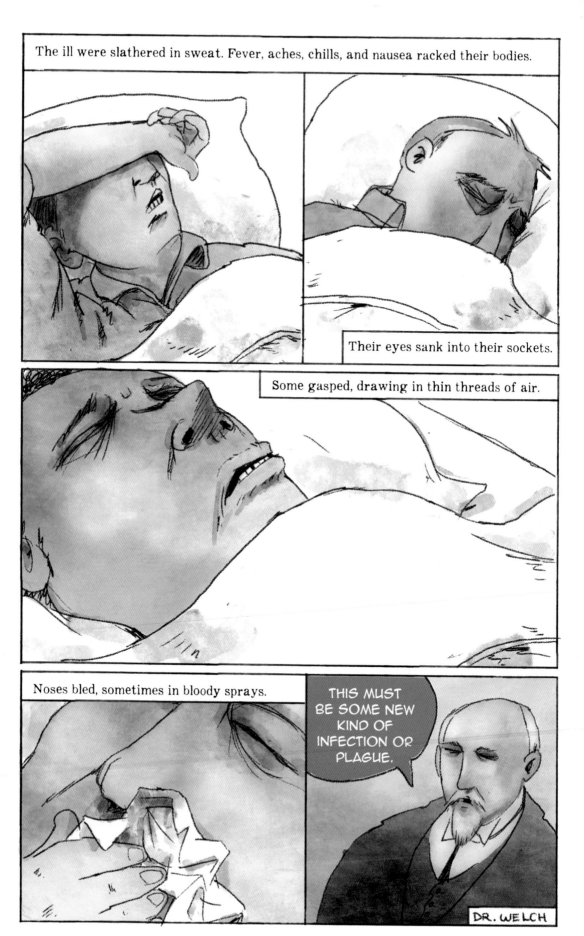

The ill were slathered in sweat. Fever, aches, chills, and nausea racked their bodies.

Their eyes sank into their sockets.

Some gasped, drawing in thin threads of air.

Noses bled, sometimes in bloody sprays.

THIS MUST BE SOME NEW KIND OF INFECTION OR PLAGUE.

DR. WELCH

By the end of September 1918, 757 soldiers had died.

The camp ran short of coffins.

Without them, the dead were "all dressed up" and laid out in long double rows in barracks made over into temporary morgues.

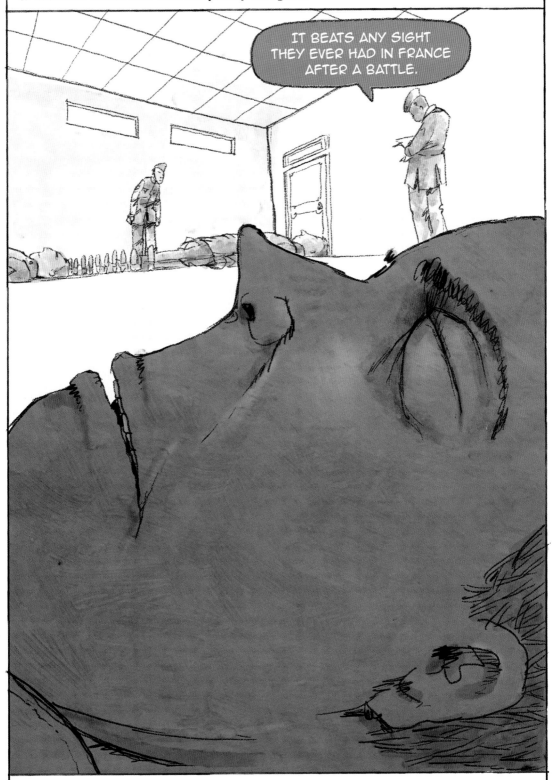

IT BEATS ANY SIGHT THEY EVER HAD IN FRANCE AFTER A BATTLE.

Were the suburbs of Boston more deadly than the killing fields of France?

Military bases filled with sick soldiers and sailors ringed Boston; there was little chance the city could avoid the disease. Still, Massachusetts Health official Dr. John Hitchcock tried to allay fears.

THE MALADY APPEARS TO BE IN THE NATURE OF THE OLD FASHION GRIPPE. . . . DAILY CASES APPEAR TO BE DIMINISHING.

He was **wrong.** A civilian flu victim entered Boston City Hospital on September 3. Soon Boston hospitals overflowed with hundreds of flu patients. Thirty-eight nurses fell ill. In some schools, four out of ten students were out sick. Within weeks, the flu claimed 334 lives.

In nearby Dorchester, the train of horse-drawn hearses clip-clopping past seven-year-old Francis Russell's home prodded his curiosity.

He followed them to the cemetery.

There he discovered "an old tent full of old boxes with handles on them."

Coffins. The cemetery couldn't dig graves fast enough and had erected a circus tent to store the waiting dead.

Back home, Francis watched girls jumping rope.

I HAD A BIRD AND HIS NAME WAS ENZA. I OPENED A WINDOW AND IN-FLU-ENZA.

Massachusetts governor Samuel McCall asked anyone with medical training to volunteer their aid. Nurses—and doctors—were in short supply, having been taken by the military for war service.

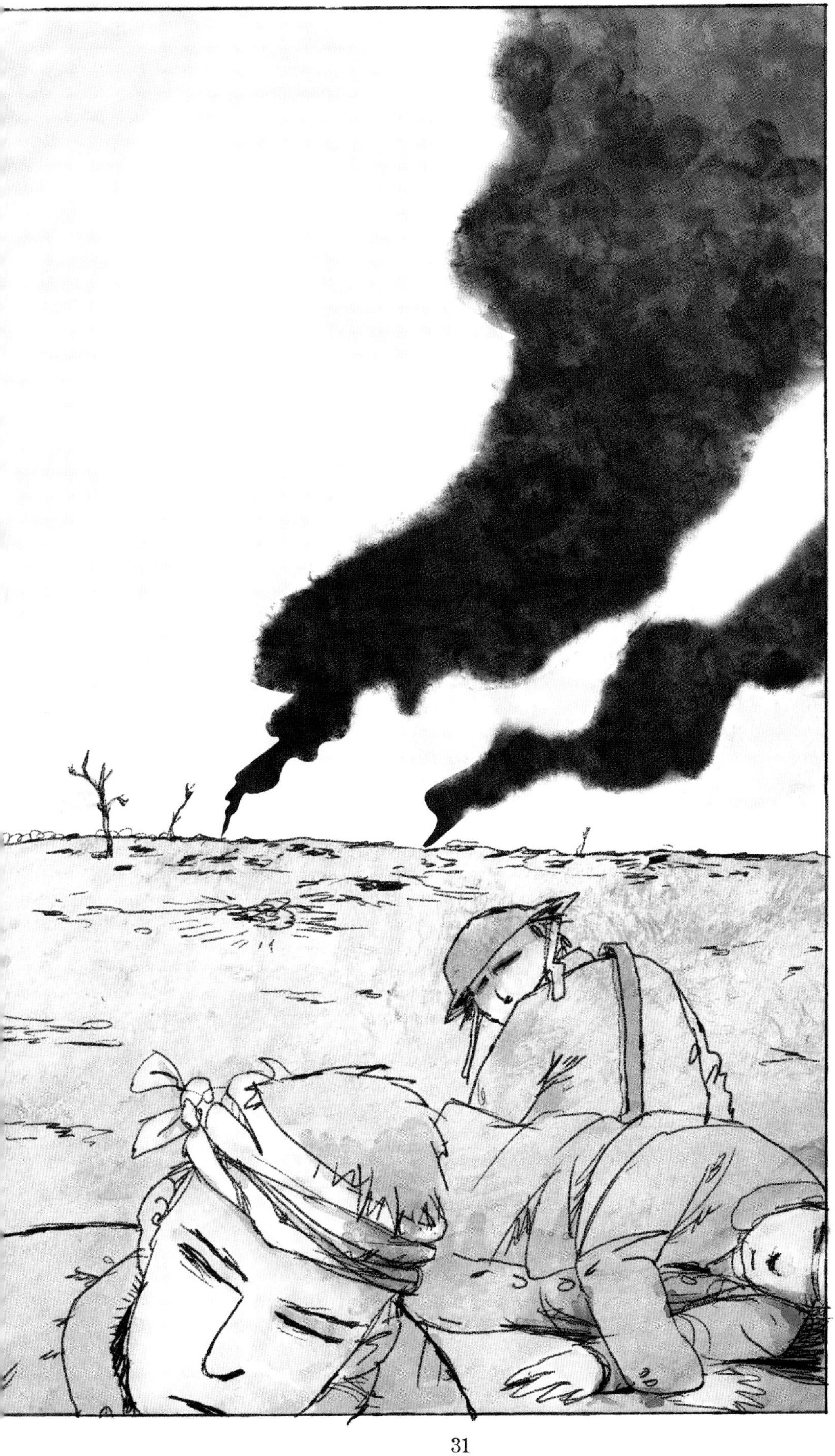

The idea that the disease spread from person to person was accepted if not fully understood. With that in mind, public leaders scrambled to meet the widening infection and closed theaters, movie houses, concert and dance halls, fraternal lodges, and schools.

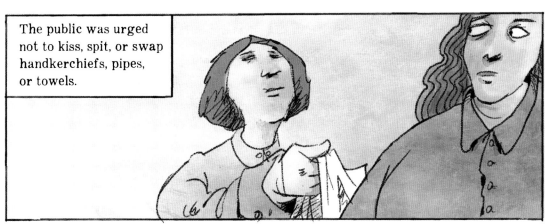

The public was urged not to kiss, spit, or swap handkerchiefs, pipes, or towels.

A month into the epidemic, almost three thousand people from Boston and surrounding communities had died.

IT SEEMED AS IF ALL THE CITY WAS DYING.

As the flu began its rampage through Boston, three hundred sailors were moved from there to the largest naval shipyard in the world: the Philadelphia Navy Yard.

Soon, six hundred sailors at the Philadelphia Navy Yard were ill. Within thirty-six hours, 1,500 soldiers at nearby Fort Dix in New Jersey were laid low.

Civilians became ill.

THERE IS NOTHING TO BE ALARMED ABOUT. I EXPECT THE DISEASE WILL BURN ITSELF OUT IN ABOUT TWO WEEKS.

A.A. CAIRNS Philadelphia BUREAU of HEALTH

Across Philadelphia, the number of sick and dying swelled. Over four thousand people were stricken by the beginning of October. Five hundred and seventy died in four days.

Yet the editors of the *Philadelphia Inquirer* suggested turning a blind eye to the tragedy.

DON'T EVEN DISCUSS IT. . . . WORRY IS WORSE THAN USELESS. . . . TALK OF CHEERFUL THINGS.

But cheerful dispositions weren't enough.

Sickness forced many from their jobs and into bed. With neither customers nor employees, many businesses and shops shut down.

Lacking enough people to properly run them, trains ran willy-nilly schedules.

The telephone system suffered.

Hundreds of ill cops, firefighters, and garbage collectors couldn't show up for work.

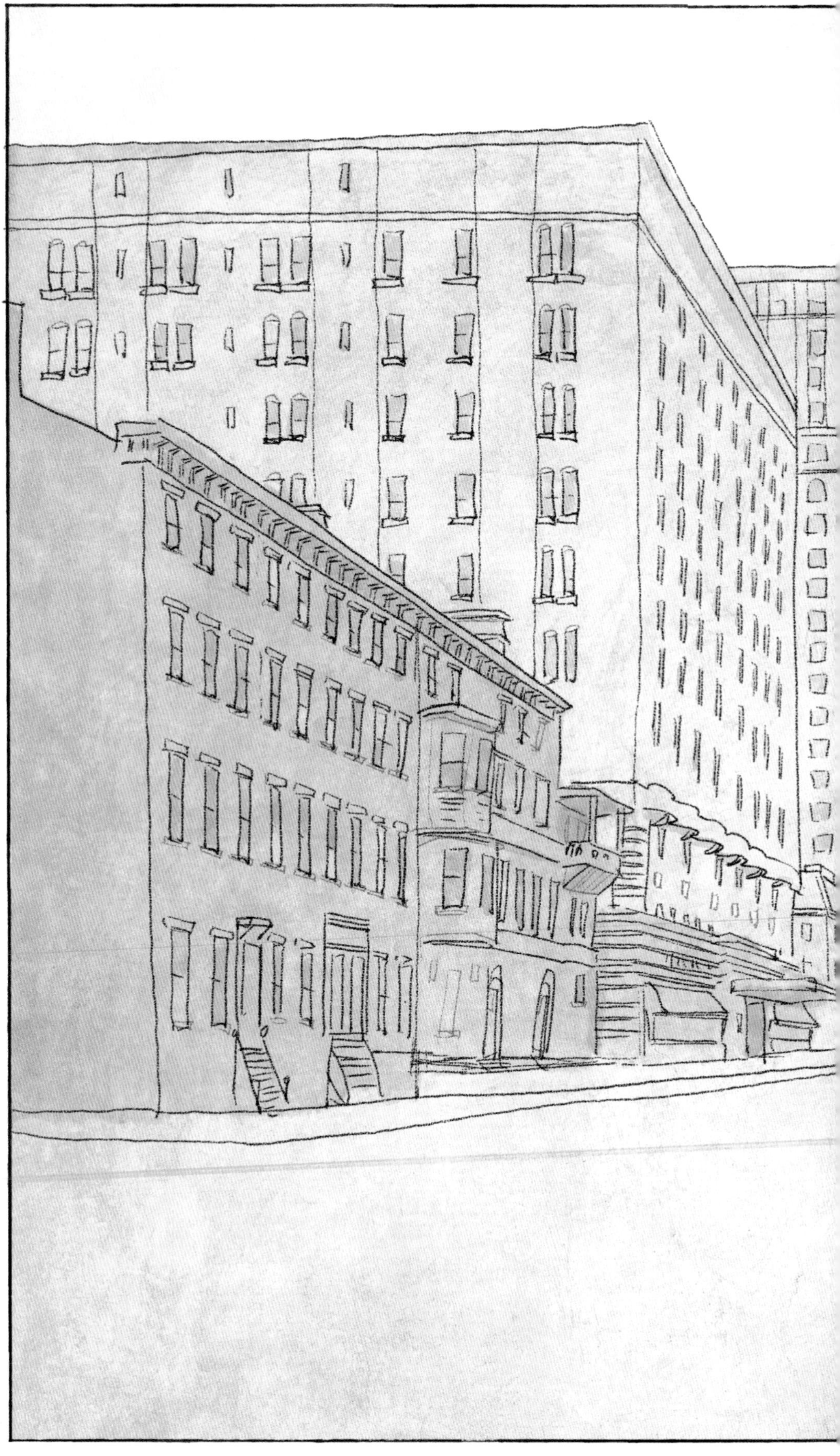

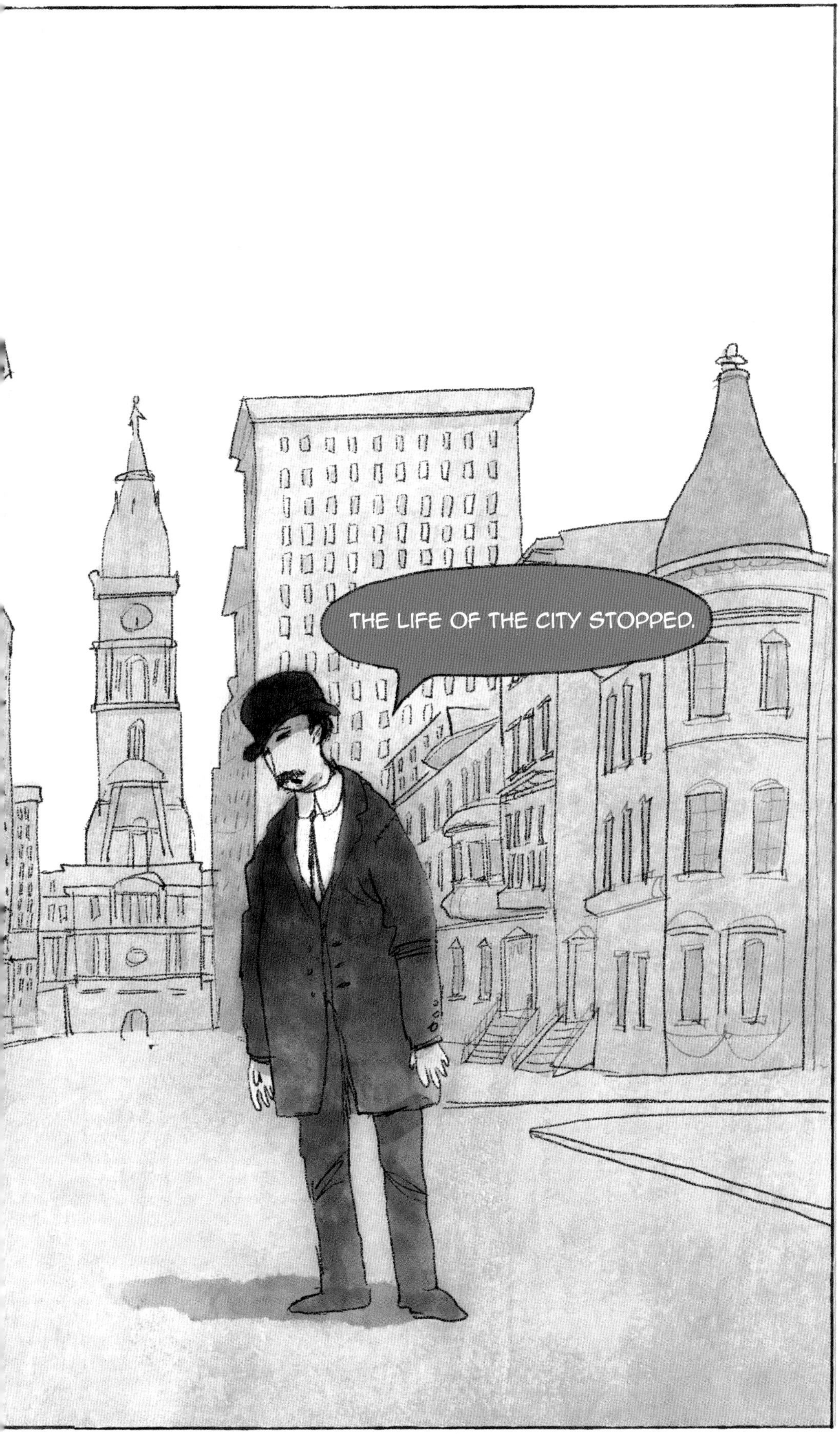
THE LIFE OF THE CITY STOPPED.

Doctors did their best, but there were too few of them; more than a quarter of Philadelphia's doctors—and nurses—were serving with the military.

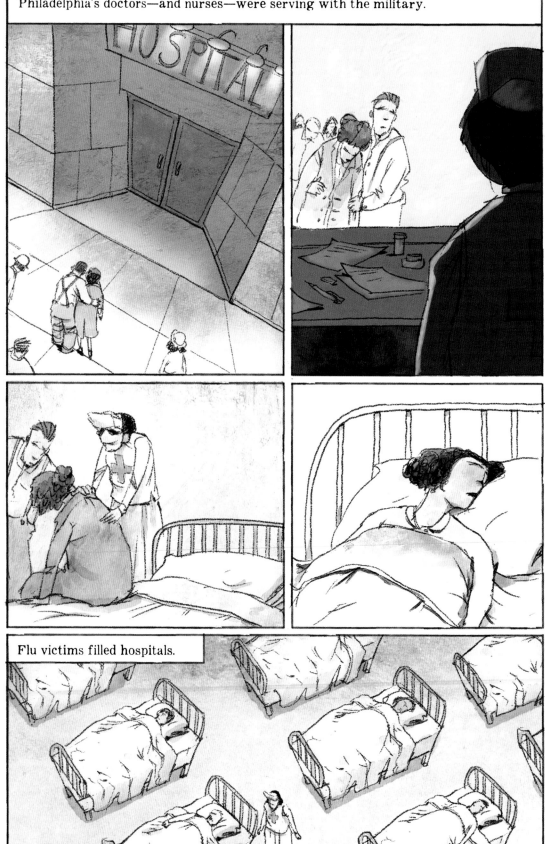

Flu victims filled hospitals.

During one week in October, the death rate was seven hundred times higher than normal. The heartbreaking tally by the end of the month was more than 11,000.

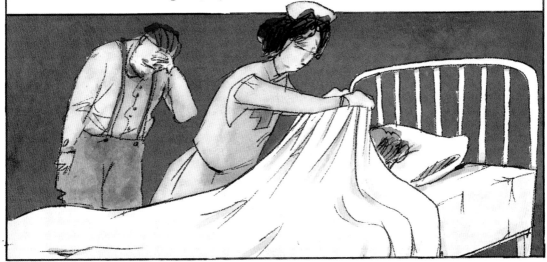

A DREADFUL BUSINESS.

And "business" was brisk. Dead bodies piled up in mortuaries. Corpses were crammed into the city morgue in stacks. Funeral parlors were overwhelmed.

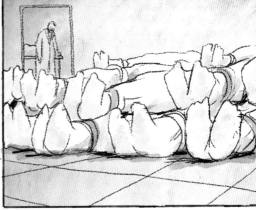

At times, morticians refused bodies, leaving surviving family members no choice but to wrap their dead in a sheet and lay them in a corner of the household.

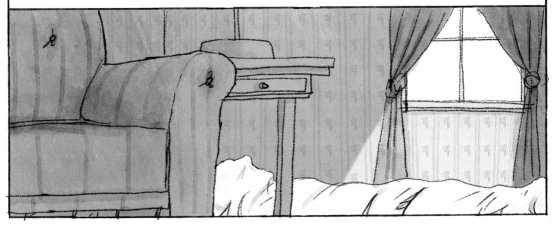

When they were able, trucks toured neighborhoods and picked up the dead.

THERE WERE NO COFFINS IN THE WAGONS, JUST BODIES PILED ON TOP OF EACH OTHER.

It reminded people of the death carts from the medieval Black Plague.

The demand for caskets outstripped supply. Funeral homes needed guards to protect their inventory.

Mourners sometimes arrived at grave-sites, discovered all the gravediggers were sick, and dug the graves them-selves.

In the closing four months of 1918, 13,426 Philadelphians died from influenza and subsequent pneumonia. A survivor remembered . . .

IT DIDN'T LAST TOO LONG.

She then reflected on the memory.

IT WAS A WHOLE LIFETIME.

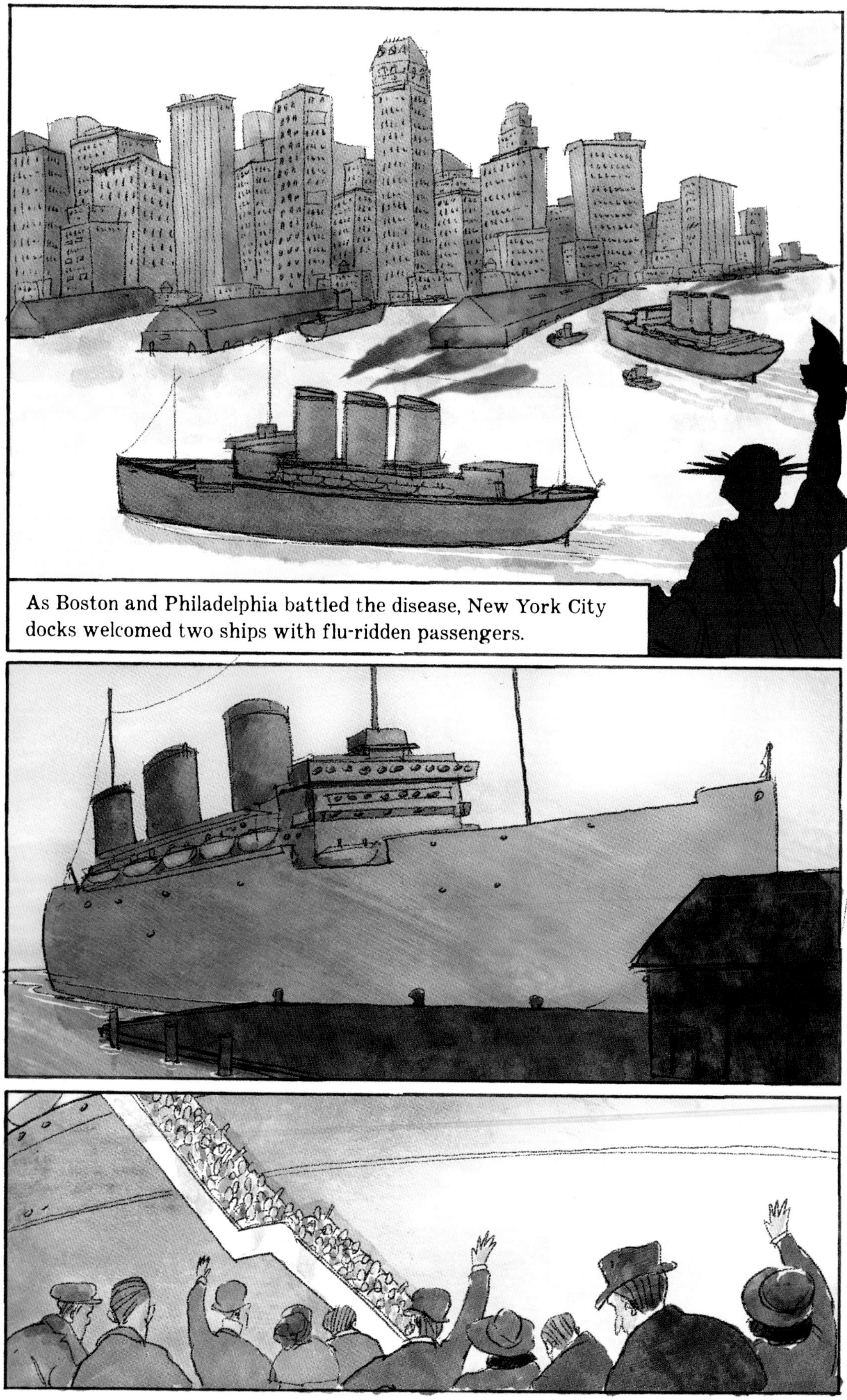
As Boston and Philadelphia battled the disease, New York City docks welcomed two ships with flu-ridden passengers.

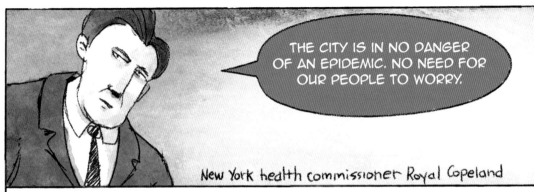

THE CITY IS IN NO DANGER OF AN EPIDEMIC. NO NEED FOR OUR PEOPLE TO WORRY.

New York health commissioner Royal Copeland

Copeland insisted the disease was in a "very mild form" or perhaps not the flu at all, but new cases of flu per day jumped from tens to hundreds to thousands.

Officials employed all kinds of ways to stop the disease.

People were fined for failing to properly clean restaurant glasses or for spitting on the street. Warnings against spitting were posted, and would remain for another sixty years.

An ocean liner landed in New York Harbor and was met by an ambulance to receive a flu-afflicted government official who had been abroad on business.

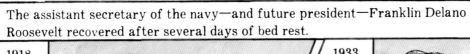

The assistant secretary of the navy—and future president—Franklin Delano Roosevelt recovered after several days of bed rest.

1918

1933

On October 1, Copeland announced the epidemic had halted. He was wrong.

Three weeks later, he predicted the worst was over. He was wrong again.

Copeland begged for hundreds of nurses, as well as orderlies and cleaning women. To help, society matrons stood on the steps of luxury Fifth Avenue shops Altman's and Tiffany's and "accosted" passersby with requests for help in the influenza fight.

Following a different path than Boston and Philadelphia, Copeland kept schools open, reasonably arguing that schools offered healthier surroundings than the cramped, dirty tenement buildings most children called home. He kept theaters open, too, as long as they were well ventilated. Subways ran, but with open windows.

ONE OF MY PRIME DUTIES WAS TO KEEP THE CITY FROM GOING MAD ON THE SUBJECT OF INFLUENZA.

By November 14, New York City's Department of Public Health had reported over 145,000 flu and pneumonia cases. About 20,000 died. Still, it was the lowest death rate—the number of dead per 100,000 people—on the East Coast.

Many Americans, boiling with disgust at their new enemy, the Germans, looked to blame them for the flu.

THE EPIDEMIC WAS STARTED BY HUNS SENT ASHORE BY BOCHE SUBMARINE COMMANDERS. . . . IT WOULD BE QUITE EASY FOR ONE OF THOSE GERMAN AGENTS TO TURN LOOSE SPANISH INFLUENZA GERMS IN A THEATER OR SOME OTHER PLACE WHERE LARGE NUMBERS OF PERSONS ARE ASSEMBLED.

Lieutenant Colonel Philip Doane, federal official

But Doane was just guessing.

Twenty-six of forty military camps around the country reported at least a quarter of their soldiers ill. Twenty thousand new cases were reported over just two days. More than 160,000 soldiers and sailors caught the flu in three weeks spanning September and October 1918.

The sickness spread beyond army camps. Forty-three states reported outbreaks.

In North Carolina, author Thomas Wolfe watched as his flu-stricken brother "gasped a thread of air into his lungs. . . . It was monstrous, brutal."

Chicago endured 38,000 influenza cases. One was a patriotic sixteen-year-old boy who joined the Red Cross Motor Corps with a mind to helping the battlefield wounded. But his plan was upset by the flu, and he spent three weeks recovering before making the trip to France. There, he practiced his cartooning, a talent that would earn Mickey Mouse creator Walt Disney fame far, far beyond his ambulance driving.

While thousands died, the disease mocked medicine's ability to defeat it. People became desperate. Something, anything had to be done . . . even quackery.

People strung bags of camphor or garlic around their necks, wore goose grease poultices . . .

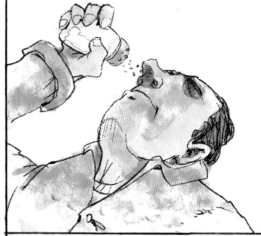

. . . and stuffed salt up their noses.

They gargled with chlorinated soda and sodium bicarbonate and boric acid. A man insisted his wife bathe in mouthwash in hope of killling the flu germs.

One doctor insisted nightcaps—head covers worn to bed—were the sure preventative for the flu.

YEARS AGO WHEN NIGHT-CAPS WERE UNIVERSALLY WORN, NO ONE EVER HAD COLDS. . . . INFLUENZA HAD NEVER BEEN HEARD OF.

Rightly or wrongly, onions earned the reputation as a near miracle drug, prompting a Pennsylvania woman to feed her eight children a diet exclusively of onion omelets, soups, and salads. When her four-year-old daughter caught the flu, an Oregon mother poured onion syrup down her throat and, for good measure, buried the girl up to her neck in raw onions for three days. She survived both the flu and the "cure."

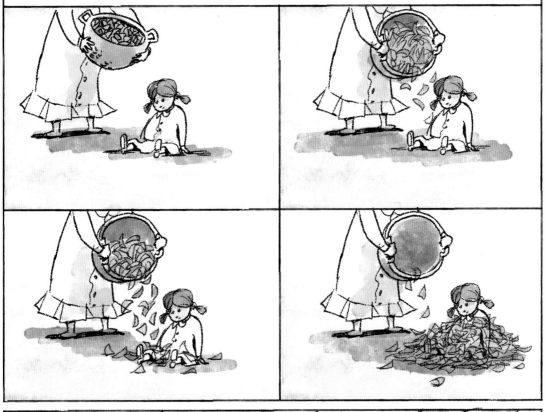

The dean of Fordham Medical School in New York offered a regime of home rest, alcohol, simple diet, and "the free use of mustard plasters and mustard footbaths."

Some people counted on the imagined powers of smoldering coal smoke mixed with sulfur or brown sugar to prevent the flu, letting the blue-green fumes fill their homes. Still others sprinkled themselves with turpentine and sugar.

One man cooked five gallons of homebrewed cure on his kitchen stove.

It wasn't real medicine but smelled and tasted the part.

EVERYBODY WAS ASKING FOR MEDICINE AND THERE WASN'T ANY.

Scientific knowledge of diseases and how they were spread was in its infancy. Understanding the link between a bacteria and a particular illness was still unfolding. And the nature of disease-causing viruses was even more perplexing. With little solid information to go on, officials relied on their intuition instead and decided dust promoted the flu.

One Colorado town used a water wagon and fire hose to dampen dirt streets. In San Francisco, the street and sewer workers were directed to flush streets and sidewalks with water.

New York City made it a crime to dry-sweep subway platforms and stairwells, promising jail time and fines for anyone ignoring the law. The Chicago health commissioner scolded school officials for dry-sweeping classrooms and hallways. Still, Surgeon General Rupert Blue—something of "America's Doctor"—warned there was . . .

NO SPECIFIC CURE FOR INFLUENZA . . . AND THAT MANY OF THE ALLEGED CURES AND REMEDIES . . . BEING RECOMMENDED BY NEIGHBORS, NOSTRUM VENDORS, AND OTHERS DO MORE HARM THAN GOOD.

A blunt New York druggist simply called users of outlandish and outrageous cures . . .

IMBECILES.

The three thousand miles separating California from the epidemic in the East barely slowed the flu's arrival. Two weeks after the outbreak at Camp Devens in Massachusetts, 35,000 Californians were sick. Scores died every day. Schools were closed.

To combat the "black wings of pestilence" hovering over San Francisco, the city's board of supervisors restricted hospitals to flu patients; all others were turned out.

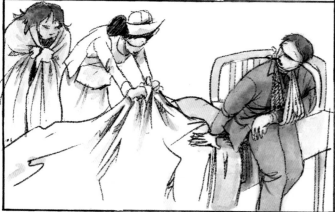

Dances and social gatherings were banned, except for church services.

On October 24, the city passed an ordinance requiring the wearing of masks.

San Francisco Mayor James "Sunny Jim" Rolph

WEAR A MASK AND SAVE YOUR LIFE! A MASK IS 99% PROOF AGAINST INFLUENZA.

Despite Mayor Rolph's assurances, there was no proof masks stopped the disease.

Even so, shirt, overalls, and other clothing factories put aside their regular work and transformed miles of cloth into masks.

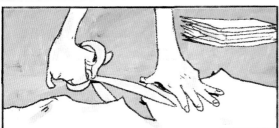

The Red Cross distributed one hundred thousand masks.

The police arrested hundreds for not wearing their masks.

But the war effort was left untouched and giant fundraising rallies, known as Liberty Loan drives, continued.

BUY BONDS

COUGH!

Masks weren't restricted to San Francisco. The nearby city of Oakland mandated masks also, and went so far as to detail three hundred special "masked cops" to enforce the rule under threat of fines and jail sentences. Neighboring Berkeley followed suit, arresting 175 "mask slackers" within days of announcing its mask ordinance.

Seattle, Washington, residents were ordered to wear masks. Streetcar conductors chased away riders without them.

In a head-scratching twist, Seattle city officials noticed that in the wake of the mask ordinance, marriage license applications plummeted and divorce applications spiked.

Back in San Francisco, the mayor said,

MASKS HAVE SAVED UNTOLD SUFFERING AND MANY DEATHS.

SAN FRANCISCO MAYOR JAMES "Sunny Jim" Rolph

But the health commissioner of Detroit was unconvinced. He thought that one hundred thousand people could be "scared into illness." He said flu masks are . . .

PURE FAKE AND "POPPY-COCK."

Detroit health commissioner James Inches

By the end of October, the flu's grip on San Francisco weakened. The order to wear masks ended at noon on November 21. Wearers tore their masks from their faces. Sidewalks were quickly strewn with gauze.

In the end, San Francisco's death rate was the worst on the West Coast. Masks could no more stop the flu germ than a chainlink fence can stop the progress of a housefly.

With hundreds of thousands of sick people across America, the demand for nurses was great.

NURSING WAS NINE-TENTHS OF THE BATTLE IN RECOVERING FROM INFLUENZA.

Philadelphia health commissioner

With the help of a nurse, scorching fevers could be cooled, food and water furnished, and rest and calm insured.

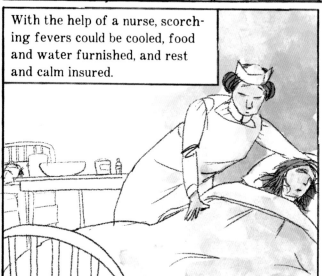

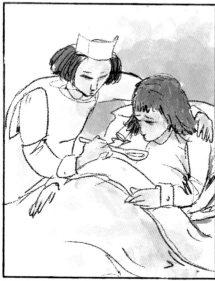

In the battle against Spanish influenza, the participation of even one nurse was important . . . and could stop a movie show.

Newly graduated nurse Josie M. Brown was ordered to work, laboring sixteen hours a day until the epidemic was over. Grim tasks accompanied the long hours.

WE WRAPPED [THE DEAD] IN A WINDING SHEET AND LEFT NOTHING BUT THE BIG TOE ON THE LEFT FOOT OUT WITH A SHIPPING TAG ON IT TO TELL THE MAN'S RANK, HIS NEAREST OF KIN, AND HOMETOWN.

Surgeon General Rupert Blue set to the difficult task of trying to find nurses and doctors. He telegraphed the American Red Cross. The group became the government's official recruiter of nurses and eventually enrolled 24,000.

Among them were Home Defense nurses who proved to be indispensable against the Spanish influenza. They were trained nurses who were ineligible to be sent overseas because of their age, marriage, or color. In spite of the shortage of nurses in Europe, trained African American nurses were denied overseas duty.

Many of the nurses endured the grueling and grim experiences of nurse Josie Brown. Hospitals overflowed. The number of patients doubled, tripled, quadrupled without a corresponding increase in nurses, who found themselves working hour after hour.

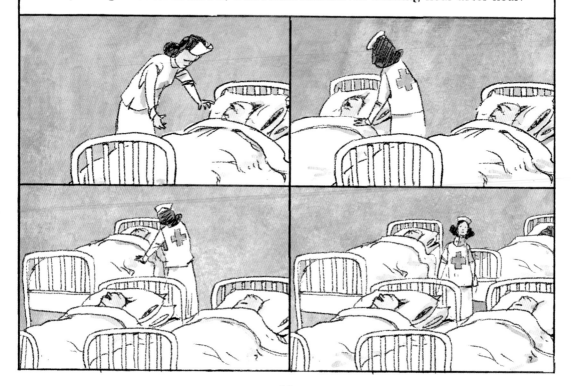

Visiting nurses served city tenements and backwoods shacks, comforting the ill and the distraught. They sponged patients, changed linens, checked temperatures, distributed food, cooked meals, and dispensed medicine.

EIGHT MILES FROM TALLADEGA [ALABAMA], IN THE BACKWOODS, A COLORED [SIC] FAMILY OF TEN WERE IN BED AND DYING FOR THE WANT OF ATTENTION. . . . I ROLLED UP MY SLEEVES AND KILLED CHICKENS AND BEGAN TO COOK. I FORGOT I WAS NOT A COOK, BUT I ONLY THOUGHT OF SAVING LIVES. I MILKED THE COW, GAVE MEDICINE, AND DID EVERYTHING I COULD TO HELP.

African American nurse Bessie B. Hawse recounted her experience:

It was selfless and vital work.

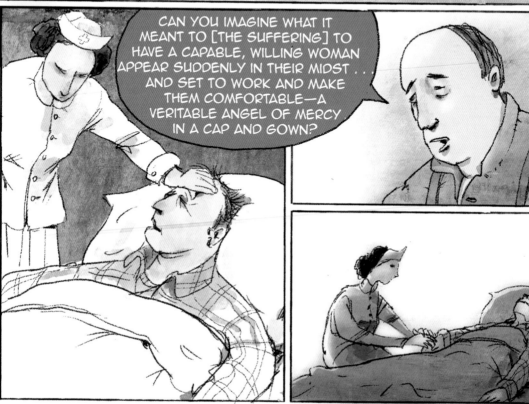

CAN YOU IMAGINE WHAT IT MEANT TO [THE SUFFERING] TO HAVE A CAPABLE, WILLING WOMAN APPEAR SUDDENLY IN THEIR MIDST . . . AND SET TO WORK AND MAKE THEM COMFORTABLE—A VERITABLE ANGEL OF MERCY IN A CAP AND GOWN?

In the absence of nurses, ordinary people ignored the risks and picked up the slack. In Durango, Colorado . . .

THE NURSES WERE SICK. SO PEOPLE, GOOD PEOPLE, JUST VOLUNTEERED.

In San Francisco, five hundred teachers volunteered and the school kitchens were dedicated to feeding the ill. In Chicago, a country club was converted into a hospital, and womens' club members volunteered to act as its nurses.

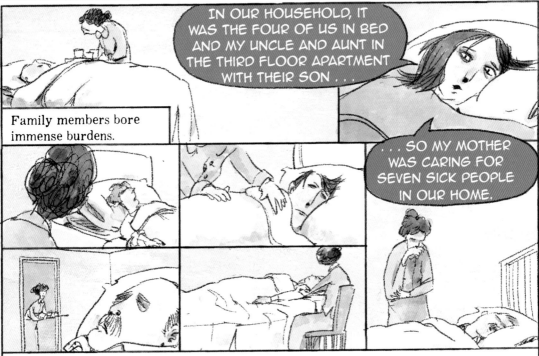

IN OUR HOUSEHOLD, IT WAS THE FOUR OF US IN BED AND MY UNCLE AND AUNT IN THE THIRD FLOOR APARTMENT WITH THEIR SON . . .

Family members bore immense burdens.

. . . SO MY MOTHER WAS CARING FOR SEVEN SICK PEOPLE IN OUR HOME.

Ignoring the risks of nursing did not make them go away. Professionals or volunteers died. Among them were 127 army nurses.

The dead piled up, but doctors didn't throw up their hands in defeat. William Park, head of the Bureau of Laboratories of New York City's Department of Public Health leaped to the challenge of concocting a vaccine for influenza.

Vaccination—infecting a person with a mild or weakened strain of disease—provided subsequent immunity from some diseases such as smallpox, and there was confidence one could be found for the flu.

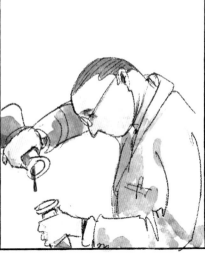

The bureau fabricated a three-dose vaccine.

On October 18, Park's boss, Health Commissioner Royal Copeland, pronounced the laboratory's vaccine "excellent" without waiting for evidence proving his assertion true. He explained it had been prepared from the Pfeiffer's bacillus or "influenza germ."

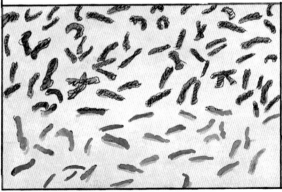

In 1892, German doctor Richard Pfeiffer had discovered the bacteria responsible for causing influenza . . .

. . . or had he?

About fifty years earlier, French chemist Louis Pasteur championed the revolutionary germ theory of disease, stating disease resulted from the attack of germs from outside the body. He said microbes caused cholera, tuberculosis, smallpox, and rabies, among others.

THE ROLE OF THE INFINITELY SMALL IN NATURE IS INFINITELY GREAT.

In 1885, a frantic mother presented Pasteur with her nine-year-old son who had been bitten by a rabid dog. Pasteur possessed a vaccine against rabies but it was untested. Knowing the boy was doomed without his help, Pasteur shrugged off his worries about the experimental vaccine and inoculated him.

The boy lived.

Other scientists followed Pasteur's pursuit of the germ theory. One was Richard Pfeiffer.

In 1892, Pfeiffer discovered the bacteria responsible for causing influenza. Or so he claimed; there was the problem that he failed to transmit the disease to test animals when he infected them with the microbe. But Pfeiffer was a renowned scientist celebrated for excellent work, and his repute carried the day. With little arm-twisting, the world convinced itself he was correct, and Pfeiffer's bacillus's link to influenza was conventional wisdom . . . right up to 1918.

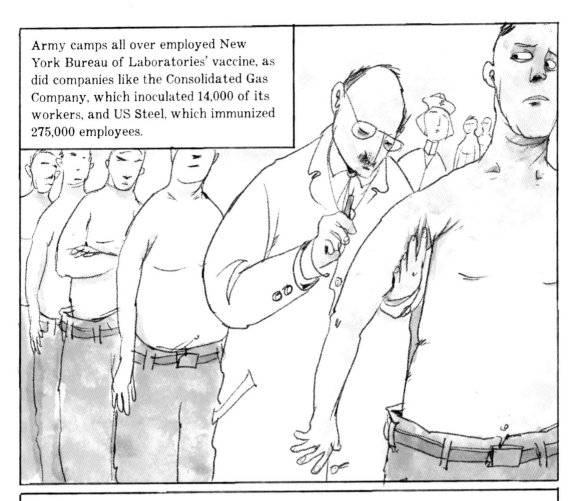

Army camps all over employed New York Bureau of Laboratories' vaccine, as did companies like the Consolidated Gas Company, which inoculated 14,000 of its workers, and US Steel, which immunized 275,000 employees.

Tufts Medical School in Boston developed their own Pfeiffer's bacillus vaccine that was widely used in San Francisco. New Orleans's Tulane University concocted their own vaccine as did the medical school of the University of Pittsburgh.

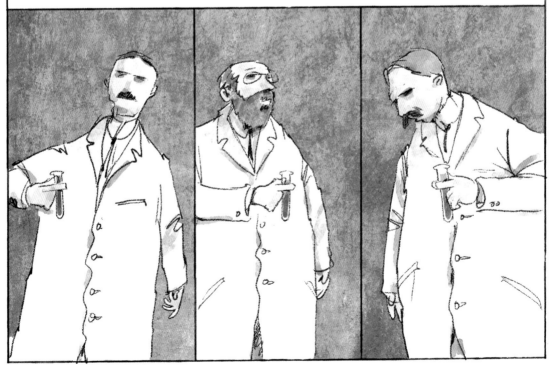

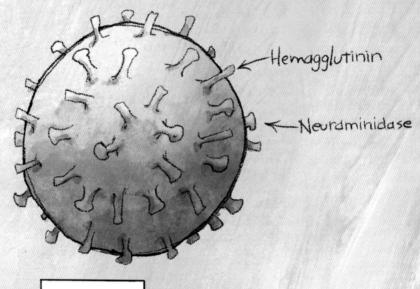

Flu Virus

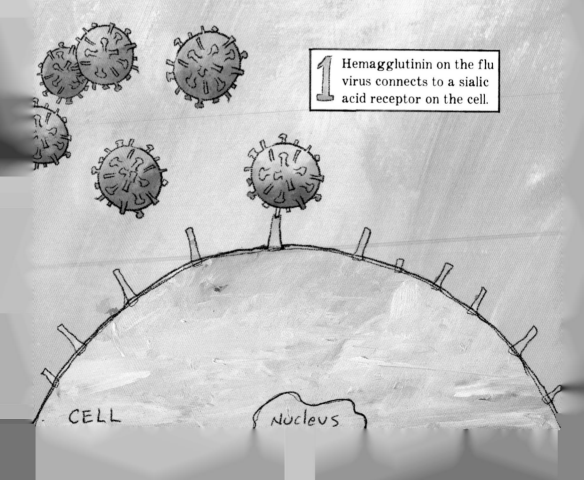

1 Hemagglutinin on the flu virus connects to a sialic acid receptor on the cell.

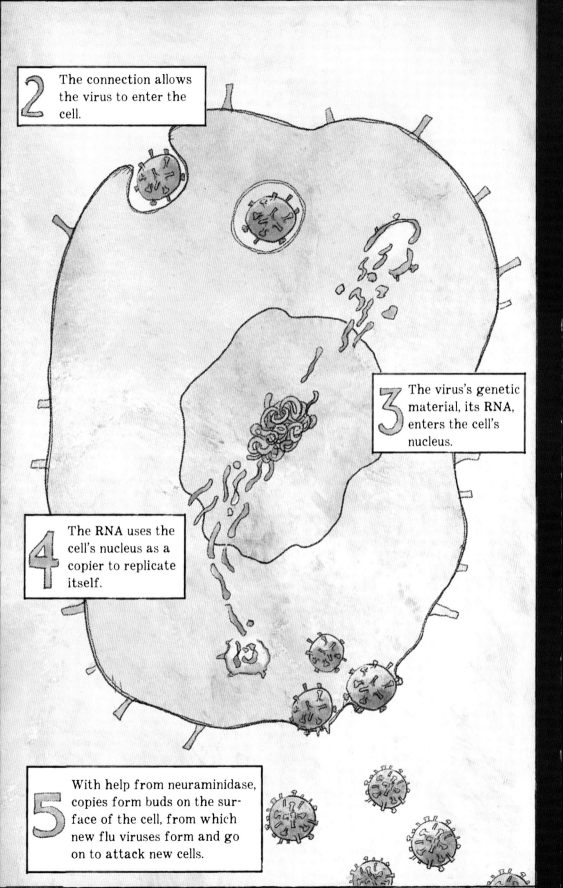

2 The connection allows the virus to enter the cell.

3 The virus's genetic material, its RNA, enters the cell's nucleus.

4 The RNA uses the cell's nucleus as a copier to replicate itself.

5 With help from neuraminidase, copies form buds on the surface of the cell, from which new flu viruses form and go on to attack new cells.

But William Park came to question the thoroughness of his work. He was troubled by not discovering Pfeiffer's bacillus in every influenza case, as would be expected. The absence of Pfeiffer's bacillus in all flu victims perplexed others as well. A naval medical officer working in Boston during the lethal epidemic had difficulty finding the bacillus in victims' throat washings and phlegm. In Chicago, a scientist reported the bacillus in only a third of influenza cases.

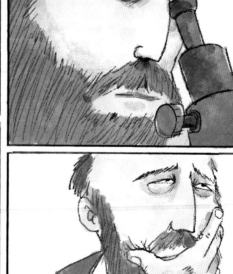

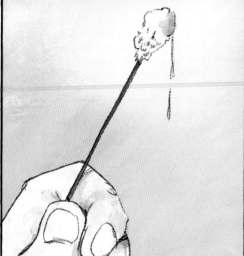

Complicating the hunt for an effective treatment was the quirky nature of the disease. Even the most casual of observers could see the Spanish flu nimbly leaped from person to person. But experiments to study the flu by explicitly transmitting it to volunteers failed again and again.

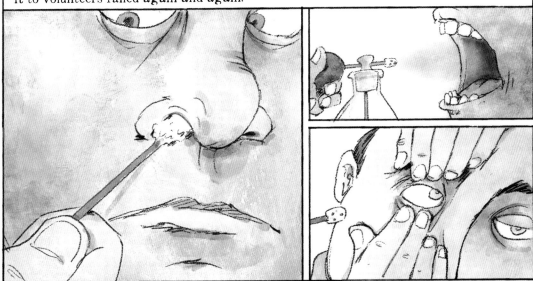

Harvard professor Dr. Milton Rosenau conducted experiments in Boston and San Francisco using 162 navy volunteers. He swabbed or sprayed Pfeiffer's bacillus into volunteers' nose, throat, and eyes. No one became ill. Some volunteers were directed to shake the hands and inhale the breath of flu victims.

Other volunteers had the messier job of receiving direct coughs in the face from an acutely sick patient. No one got sick.

"Doctors know no more about this flu than fourteenth-century Florentine doctors had known about the Black Death," groused a scientist.

PERHAPS, IF WE LEARNED ANYTHING, IT IS THAT WE ARE NOT QUITE SURE WHAT WE KNOW ABOUT THE DISEASE.

Dr. Milton Rosenau

The dying continued.

Flu-born tragedy circled the globe in a widespread contagion known as a pandemic. Its movement from place to place was almost nonsensical.

Mumbai, India, was at opposite ends of the earth from New York City, yet the flu peaked in both cities in the same week.

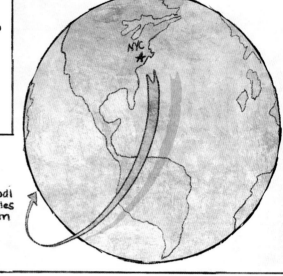

Mumbai
7,800 miles
12,500 km

A continent away from the East Coast outbreak, the West Coast cities of Seattle, Los Angeles, and San Francisco saw the epidemic peak before nearby eastern Pittsburgh.

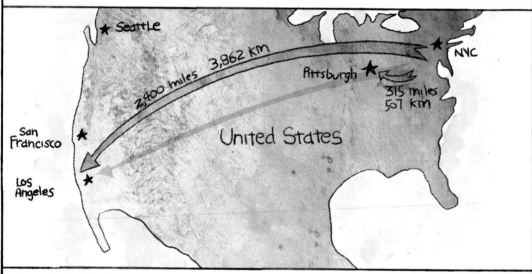

★ Seattle

2,400 miles 3,862 km

Pittsburgh ★

NYC ★

315 miles
507 km

San Francisco ★

United States

Los Angeles ★

It took the flu three weeks to spread a mere eighty miles across a slice of Connecticut.

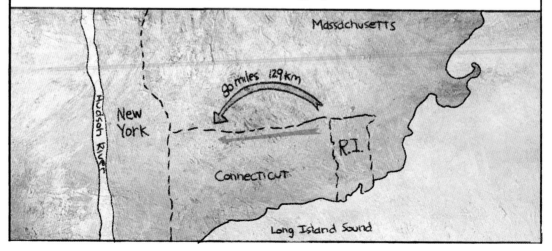

Massachusetts

80 miles 129 km

Hudson River

New York

R.I.

Connecticut

Long Island Sound

In India, the flu killed upwards of 17 million people. Streets were littered with the dead and dying. Corpses were burned in funeral pyres.

When supplies of firewood were exhausted, bodies were put into rivers, clogging them.

The flu struck Indian nationalist leader Mahatma Gandhi, but he survived and went on to lead India to its independence from Great Britain in 1947.

The epidemic swept over South Africa and infected half the population. In Cape Town, empty, silent streets and shops suggested a "city of the dead."

In Austria, Expressionist painter Egon Schiele sketched his pregnant wife as she lay in bed, consumed by the flu. Her death portrait was his last work.

He died of influenza three days later.

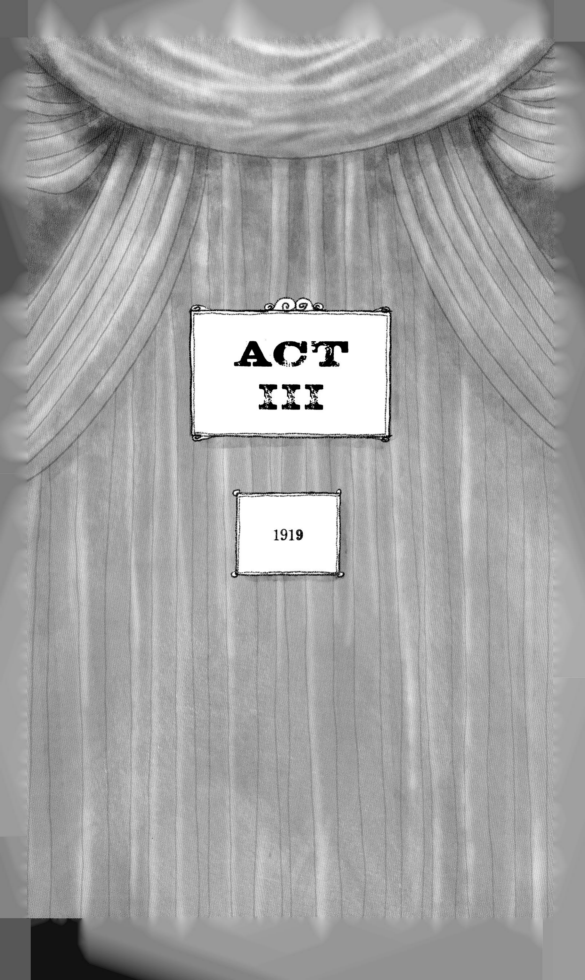

ACT
III

1919

The disease proved to be a six-to-eight-week event, running its course faster in crowded army camps. The number of cases dropped off. But like campfire embers that suddenly burst back into flames, the flu reignited in 1919.

Paris, France, saw the epidemic wane at the close of 1918, and then it flooded back in at the start of 1919. It struck as the world's most important leaders were attending the peace conference ending the Great War.

Both British prime minister David Lloyd George and French prime minister Georges Clemenceau had survived mild cases of influenza.

In the evening of April 3, American president Woodrow Wilson was seized with violent coughs, had trouble breathing, and could barely walk. His temperature spiked to 103 degrees.

British leader Lloyd George noted Wilson's "nervous and spiritual breakdown in the middle of the conference."

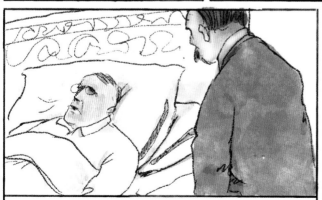

Wilson's doctor and trusted aide, Cary Grayson, said it was influenza.

It's likely Wilson wouldn't have disagreed with other survivors who counted the flu as the worst sickness they'd ever endured.

I GOT TO THE POINT WHERE I DIDN'T CARE WHETHER I DIED OR NOT.

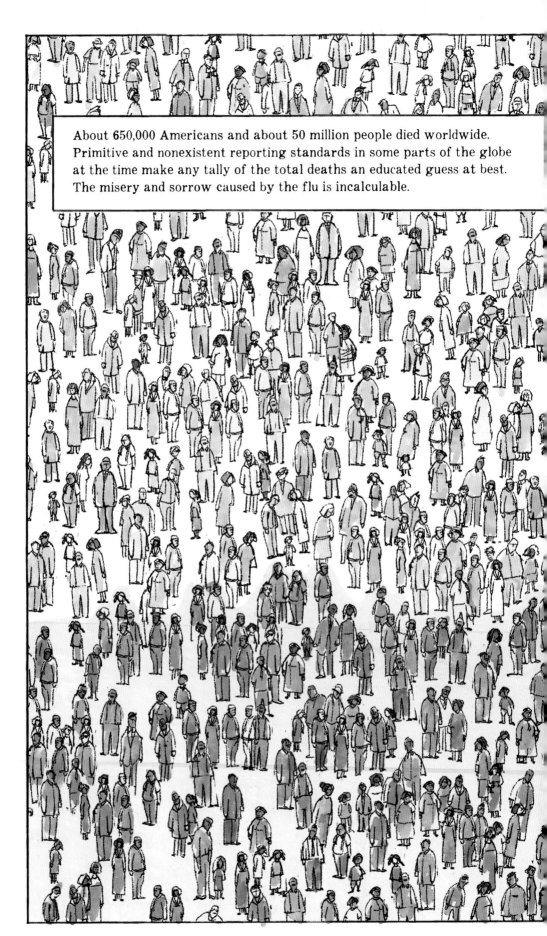

About 650,000 Americans and about 50 million people died worldwide. Primitive and nonexistent reporting standards in some parts of the globe at the time make any tally of the total deaths an educated guess at best. The misery and sorrow caused by the flu is incalculable.

One-third of the world had been infected.

No one could say exactly what killed all those millions of people.

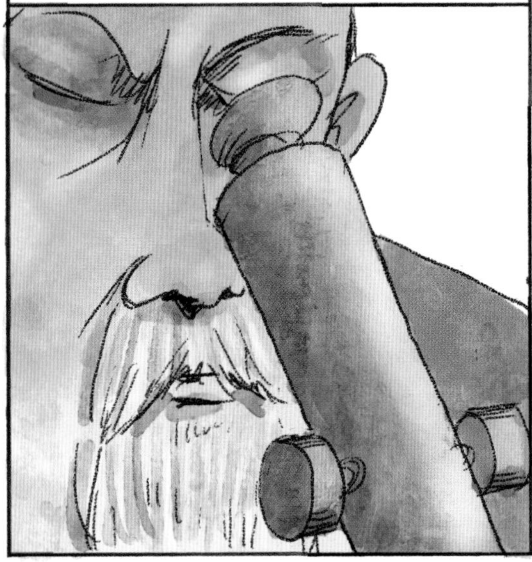

It was not Pfeiffer's bacillus.

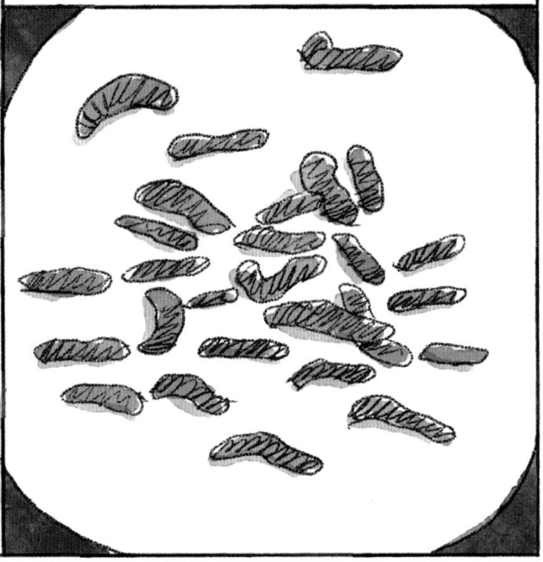

If not Pfeiffer's bacillus, then what? Discovering the cause was a knotty problem. By 1920, the eminent Dr. Welch surveyed the sad state of influenza research and said . . .

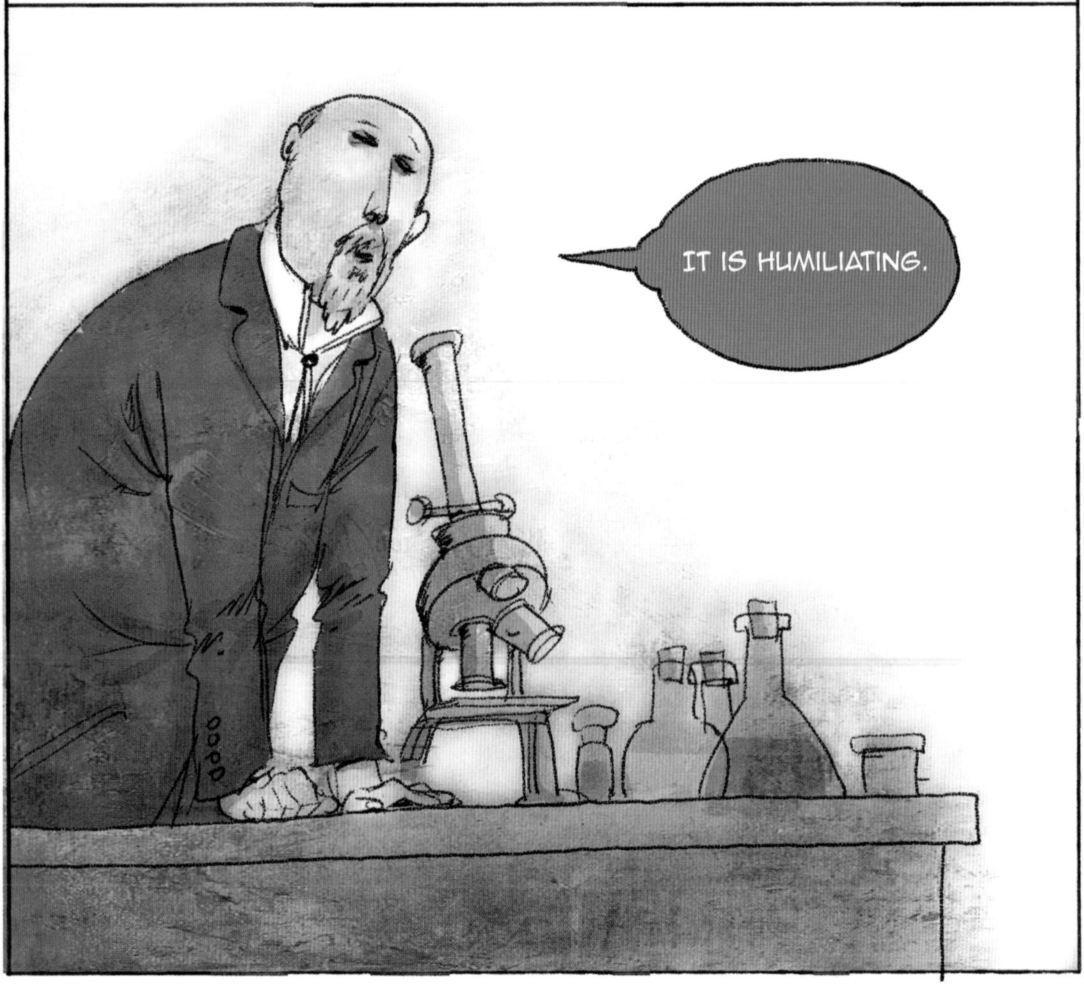
IT IS HUMILIATING.

Then a tough-minded American scientist Richard Shope became intrigued by influenza in pigs, a disease that mirrored the human variety.

During the height of the Spanish flu outbreak, an inspector of the US Bureau of Animal Industry had noticed . . .

With the knowledge of pig flu in mind, Dr. Shope conducted a series of experiments in which he passed mucus from flu-sickened pigs' noses—pig snot—through a fine, fine filter to remove all bacteria but still allow much tinier viruses through. Using the filtrated snot, he infected healthy pigs.

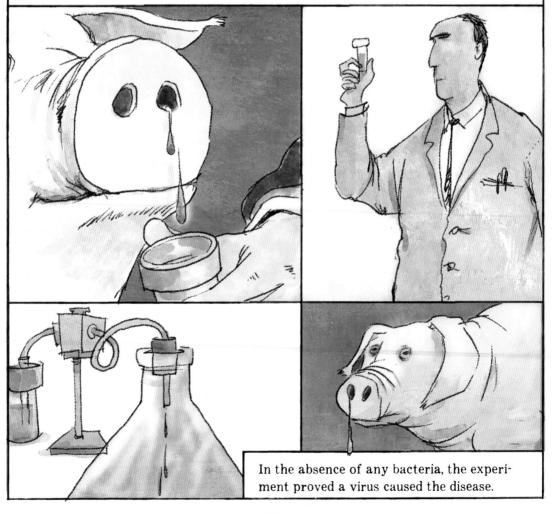

In the absence of any bacteria, the experiment proved a virus caused the disease.

If a virus caused influenza in pigs, then it stood to reason that a virus was the cause of influenza in humans. In 1933, three British scientists Wilson Smith, Christopher H. Andrewes, and Patrick Laidlaw used bacteria-free filtrated fluids—mucus and such—from human influenza victims to infect ferrets, an animal possessing the unlikely ability to catch human flu.

Sick ferrets then transmitted the flu to healthy ones.

Along the way, they even proved a sick ferret could infect a human when one of the animals sneezed in Wilson Smith's face. The evidence pointed to a virus as the cause for influenza.

However, recognizing a virus as influenza's pathogen—agent of disease—didn't explain the peculiar deadliness of the Spanish influenza. But the chance to solve the mystery seemed to disappear with the exit of the disease.

Then the overlapping paths of a soldier from 1918 and a scientist in 1995 helped solve the mystery.

In 1918, twenty-one-year-old Roscoe Vaughan was one of 43,000 soldiers at Camp Jackson in South Carolina. Vaughan never made it to a World War I battlefield.

Instead, he gasped his life away from influenza and died at 6:30 a.m. on September 26.

An army doctor performed an autopsy to confirm the cause of death.

He removed a sliver of Vaughan's diseased lung and sealed it in paraffin, a kind of wax.

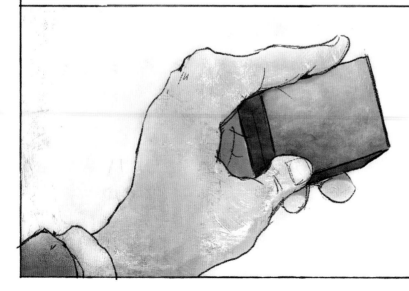

The paraffin block was sent to the Army Medical Museum where it was shelved . . .

. . . and forgotten for about eighty years.

In 1995, scientist Jeffery Taubenberger recovered Vaughan's sample and found incomplete bits of the Spanish flu virus still lurking within it. He spent years studying its genetic code, sure that within it was the secret of the virus's deadliness.

In 2005, scientist Terrence Tumpey expanded on Taubenberger's research to recreate the Spanish flu, making the unique monster whole again since its killing spree nearly a century earlier.

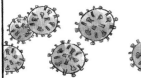

The virus easily killed lab animals. "I literally felt a chill go down my spine," Tumpey said.

Should it have been recreated?

EXPERTS ARGUE THAT WE NEED TO LEARN AS MUCH AS WE CAN . . . TO DEVELOP ANTIVIRAL DRUGS, VACCINES, AND STRATEGIES TO WARD OFF ANY NEW PANDEMIC.

UNDERSTANDING AS MUCH AS POSSIBLE ABOUT THE VIRUS THAT CAUSED THE DEVASTATING 1918–1919 INFLUENZA PANDEMIC IS AN URGENT IMPERATIVE AS WE PURSUE EFFORTS TO PREPARE FOR—AND POSSIBLY THWART—THE NEXT FLU PANDEMIC.

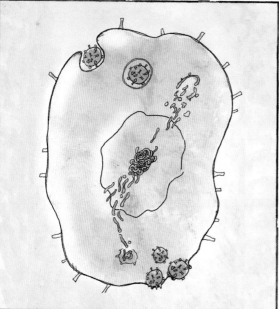

WHO'S TO SAY THE 1918 FLU COULDN'T GET OUT, EITHER BY INTENTIONAL OR UNINTENTIONAL MEANS?

RELEASE OF A HIGHLY COMMUNICABLE AND DEADLY BIOLOGICAL VIRUS COULD KILL TENS OF MILLIONS, WITH SOME ESTIMATES IN THE HUNDREDS OF MILLIONS.

Is there a right answer?

EPILOGUE

It was a three-act tragedy.

ACT ONE: The flu arrived in early 1918 and struck people across America, Europe, and perhaps Asia. It sickened many but killed few, or more accurately, it killed roughly no more than a normal flu epidemic would be expected to kill.

The details of its origin are still debated today. Evidence suggests it first appeared in the western United States, but not all researchers agree. Possibly, the virus originated in the intestines of a wild aquatic bird, a common host for the influenza microbe. Droppings from the bird infected domestic chickens, ducks, and eventually people. Or the microbe moved from domestic poultry to pigs, who transformed the virus into a new strain that infected people. The concentration and transportation of soldiers during the Great War assisted the spread of the virus.

ACT TWO: By August, a brutal strain of flu ravaged the globe, killing with a virulence twenty-five times more deadly than ordinary influenza, coupled with a perverse lethality to young adults who fell victim in greater numbers than others. Women were more likely to be stricken than men. Why young people and women were targeted is unclear.

ACT THREE: The killer made another appearance in early 1919 before the curtain came down. Unfortunately, the deadly strain of the disease made several notable, unwanted curtain calls from 1920 through 1922 before fading away. For those it touched, the Spanish influenza's grip was fierce and enduring. It brought author Katherine Anne Porter close to death and killed her fiancé. She said,

IT SIMPLY DIVIDED MY LIFE, CUT ACROSS IT LIKE THAT. SO THAT EVERYTHING BEFORE THAT WAS JUST GETTING READY, AND AFTER THAT I WAS IN SOME STRANGE WAY ALTERED, REALLY.

A doctor offered a chilling remembrance of the Spanish influenza years after he encountered it at Camp Devens:

IT SEEMED THAT NATURE GATHERED TOGETHER ALL HER STRENGTH AND DEMONSTRATED TO MAN HOW PUNY AND INSIGNIFICANT HE AND HIS FORCE ARE.

SOURCE NOTES

12 *"For it began"*: Cunha, "Influenza," 4.

21 *"Two hours after admission"*: PBS/American Experience, "A Letter from Camp Devens." www.pbs.org/wgbh/americanexperience/features/influenza-letter. Accessed May 19, 2018.

26 *"This must be"*: Byerly, *Fever of War*, 75.

27 *"all dressed up"*: PBS/American Experience, "A Letter from Camp Devens."
"It beats any sight": Ibid.

28 *"The malady appears"*: *Boston Globe*, "Fear Influenza Outbreak Among Sailors May Spread," September 6, 1918.

29 *"an old tent"*: Russell, "Journal of the Plague," 234.
"I had a bird": Ibid., 235.

33 *"It seemed as if"*: University of Michigan, "Boston, Massachusetts." *Influenza Enyclopedia*. www.influenzaarchive.org/cities/city-boston.html. Accessed January 29, 2019.

35 *"There is nothing"*: *Philadelphia Inquirer*, "Spanish Influenza Epidemic Waning," September 23, 1918.
"Don't even discuss it": *Philadelphia Inquirer*, October 5, 1918.

39 *"The life of the city"*: Barry, *The Great Influenza*, 227.

41 *"A dreadful business"*: Starr, "Influenza in 1918."

43 *"There were no coffins"*: Iezzoni, *Influenza 1918*, 135.
"It didn't last too long": Hardy, "I Remember When."
"It was a whole lifetime": Ibid.

45 *"The city is in no danger"*: PBS/American Experience, "Influenza Across America in 1918" (timeline). www.pbs.org/wgbh/americanexperience/features/influenza-timeline. Accessed May 19, 2018.
"very mild form": Ibid.

49 *"One of my prime duties"*: *New York Times*, "Epidemic Lessons Against Next Time," November 17, 1918.

50 *"The epidemic was started"*: *New York Times*, "Think Influenza Came in U-Boat," September 19, 1918.

51 *"gasped a thread of air"*: Wolfe, *Look Homeward, Angel*, 441.

52 *"Years ago when nightcaps"*: *Literary Digest*, "Back to the Night Cap," 29.

53 *"the free use"*: *New York Times*, "Influenza Cases Drop 305 in the City," September 21, 1918.

54 *"You could smell"*: PBS/American Experience, "Influenza 1918."

55 *"Everybody was asking"*: Ibid.
"No specific cure": *Atlanta Constitution*, "Warning to Public About Gripe Cures," October 27, 1918, 10.
"Imbeciles": *Boston Globe*, "Camphor and Spanish Influenza," October 16, 1918.

56 *"black wings of pestilence"*: University of Michigan, "San Francisco, California." *Influenza Encyclopedia*. www.influenzaarchive.org/cities/city-sanfrancisco.html. Accessed February 7, 2019.

57 *"Wear a mask"*: San Francisco Chronicle, "Don Masks! Rolph Urges as Best Means of Avoiding Risks," October 22, 1918.

59 *"Masks have saved"*: Online Archive of California/UCLA, "Collection of Personal Narratives."
"scared into illness": Chicago Tribune, "Jury to Pass on Masks and Lid on Fighting 'Flu,'" December 13, 1918.
"Pure fake and 'poppycock'": Ibid.

60 *"Nursing was nine-tenths"*: Morrisey, "The Influenza Epidemic of 1918," 13.

61 *"We wrapped [the dead]"*: Wedeking, "A Winding Sheet," 18.

63 *"Eight miles"*: Keeling, "'Alert to the Necessities,'" 112.

64 *"Can you imagine"*: Phillips and Killingray, *Spanish Influenza Pandemic*, 63.

65 *"The nurses were sick"*: San Francisco Chronicle, "City Teachers Volunteer," October 25, 1918.
"In our household": PBS/American Experience, "Influenza 1918."
"So my mother": Ibid.

68 *"The role of the infinitely small"*: Argüelles, "The Early Days of the Nobel Prize."

73 *"Doctors know no more"*: Barry, *The Great Influenza*, 403.
"Perhaps, if we learned": Eyler, "The State of Science," 35.

75 *"city of the dead"*: Phillips, *Epidemic*, 73.

79 *"nervous and spiritual breakdown"*: Iezzoni, *Influenza 1918*, 191.
"I got to the point": Bristow, "'It's as Bad as Anything Can Be.'"

82 *"It is humiliating"*: Barry, *The Great Influenza*, 409.

83 *"The similarity of the epidemic"*: Shope, "Influenza," 172.

87 *"I literally felt"*: Shreeve, "Why Revive a Deadly Flu Virus?"

88 *"Experts argue that"*: PBS/NOVA, "Reviving the Virus."
"Understanding as much": Ibid.
"Who's to say": Ibid.
"Release of a highly communicable": Ibid.

89 *"It simply divided"*: Porter, *Pale Horse, Pale Rider*, 694.

90 *"It seemed that nature"*: Vaughan, "The 1922 Influenza Outbreak," 1.

BIBLIOGRAPHY

BOOKS

Barry, John M. *The Great Influenza: The Story of the Deadliest Pandemic in History*. New York: Penguin Books, 2005.

Barton, Larry L., and Diana E. Northup. *Microbial Ecology*. Hoboken: Wiley-Blackwell, 2011.

Bristow, Nancy K. *American Pandemic: The Lost Worlds of the 1918 Influenza Epidemic*. New York: Oxford University Press, 2012.

Britt, Ruby Brown. *Of Harvest and Home: A Small Town Georgia Heritage*. Self-published, 1st Book Library, 2001.

Byerly, Carol R. *Fever of War: The Influenza Epidemic in the U.S. Army During World War I*. New York: New York University Press, 2005.

Collier, Richard. *The Plague of the Spanish Lady: The Influenza Pandemic of 1918–1919*. New York: Atheneum, 1974.

Crawford, Dorothy H. *Viruses: A Very Short Introduction*. New York: Oxford University Press, 2011.

Crosby, Alfred W. *America's Forgotten Pandemic: The Influenza of 1918*. New York: Cambridge University Press, 1989.

De Kruif, Paul. *Microbe Hunters*. San Diego: Harcourt Brace Jovanovich, 1954.

Dobell, Clifford. *Antony van Leeuwenhoek and His "Little Animals."* New York: Harcourt, Brace and Company, 1932. Accessed January 29, 2019.

Duncan, Kirsty. *Hunting The 1918 Flu: One Scientist's Search for a Killer Virus*. Toronto: University of Toronto Press, 2006.

Flexner, Simon, and James Thomas Flexner. *William Henry Welch and the Heroic Age of American Medicine*. New York: Viking Press, 1941.

Franck, Dan. *Bohemian Paris: Picasso, Modigliani, Matisse, and the Birth of Modern Art*. London: Weidenfeld & Nicolson, 2001.

Higgins, James E. "Keystone of an Epidemic: Pennsylvania's Urban Experience During the 1918–1919 Influenza Epidemic." PhD diss., Lehigh University, April 22, 2009.

Iezzoni, Lynette. *Influenza 1918: The Worst Epidemic in American History*. New York: TV Books, 1999.

"Influenza in Alaska: A Joint Resolution for Relief in Alaska," S.J. 199, 65th Cong., 3rd Session, 1919. Accessed January 29, 2019.

Johnson, Niall. *Britain and the 1918–19 Influenza Pandemic: A Dark Epilogue*. London, Routledge, 2006.

Kolata, Gina. *Flu: The Story of the Great Influenza Pandemic of 1918 and the Search for the Virus That Caused It*. New York: Touchstone, 1999.

Murphy, Jim. *An American Plague: The True and Terrifying Story of the Yellow Fever Epidemic of 1793*. New York: Clarion Books, 2003.

Pettit, Dorothy A., and Janice Bailie. *A Cruel Wind: Pandemic Flu in America 1918–1920*. Murfreesboro, TN: Timberlane Books, 2009.

Phillips, Howard. *Epidemic: The Story of South Africa's Five Most Lethal Human Diseases*. Athens, OH: Ohio University Press, 2012.

Phillips, Howard, and David Killingray, eds. *The Spanish Influenza Pandemic 1918–19*: New Perspectives. London: Routledge, 2003.

Porter, Katherine Anne. *Pale Horse, Pale Rider*. Orlando: Harcourt Brace Jovanovich, 1963.

Swan, John, MD. *The Entire Works of Dr. Thomas Sydenham*. London, 1742. Accessed January 29, 2019.

Taylor, Martha R., Eric J. Simon, Jean L. Dickey, Kelly A. Hogan, and Jane B. Reece. *Campbell Biology: Concepts & Connections*, 9th ed. Boston: Pearson, 2017.

Vaughan, Victor. *A Doctor's Memories*. Indianapolis: Bobbs-Merrill Company, 1926. Accessed January 29, 2019.

Wolfe, Thomas. *Look Homeward, Angel*. New York: Scribner, 1929.

PERIODICALS

Achenbach, Joel. "Can We Stop the Next Killer Flu?" *Washington Post Magazine*, December 11, 2005, W10.

Adams, Rex. "The Spanish Influenza, Berkeley's 'Quinta Columna,'" *Chronicle of the University of California*, Spring 1998. Accessed January 29, 2019.

American Journal of Public Health, vol. 10 (1920).

American Public Health Association. "Resolutions Adopted by the Section on Vital Statistics, December 11, 1918." *American Journal of Public Health*, vol. IX (1919). Accessed January 29, 2019.

Atlanta Constitution, October 27, 1918, 10.

Barry, John. "Pandemics: Avoiding the Mistakes of 1918." *Nature*, vol. 459 (May 21, 2009): 324–25.

Birmingham News (AL), October 18, 1918.

Boston Globe (various)

Bristow, Nancy K. "'It's as Bad as Anything Can Be': Patients, Identity, and the Influenza Pandemic." *Public Health Reports*, vol. 125, suppl. 3 (2010): 134–44. Accessed January 29, 2019.

Brundage, John F., and G. Dennis Shanks. "Pathogenic Reponses Among Young Adults During the 1918 Influenza Pandemic." *Emerging Infectious Diseases*, vol. 18, no. 2 (February 2012): 201.

Byerly, Carol R. "The U.S. Military and the Influenza Pandemic of 1918–1919." *Public Health Reports*, vol. 125, suppl. 3 (2010): 82–91. Accessed January 29, 2019.

Carbonate Chronicle (Leadville, CO)

Chicago Tribune (various)

Colfax Chronicle (LA), November 9, 1918.

Cunha, Burke A., MD. "Influenza: Historical Aspect of Epidemics and Pandemics." *Infectious Disease Clinics of North America*, vol. 18 (2004): 141–55. Accessed January 29, 2019.

Erkoreka, Anton. "Origins of the Spanish Influenza Pandemic (1918–1920) and Its Relation to the First World War." *Journal of Molecular and Genetic Medicine*, vol. 3, no. 2 (December 2009): 190–94.

Eyler, John M. "The State of Science, Microbiology, and Vaccines Circa 1918." *Public Health Reports*, vol. 125, suppl. 3 (2010): 27–36. Accessed January 29, 2019.

Fincher, Jack. "America's Deadly Rendezvous with the 'Spanish Lady.'" *Smithsonian*, vol. 19, no. 10 (January 1989): 130–47.

Flexner, Simon. "Obituary of Dr. William Welch." *Bulletin of the New York Academy of Medicine*, vol. 10, no. 6 (June 1934): 384–88. Accessed January 29, 2019.

Fort Collins Weekly, October 11, 1918, 4.

Frost, W. H. "The Epidemiology of Influenza." *Public Health Reports*, vol. 34, no. 33 (August 15, 1919). Accessed January 29, 2019.

Goldsmith, C. S., and S. E. Miller. "Modern Uses of Electron Microscopy for Detection of Viruses." *Clinical Microbiology Reviews*, vol. 22, no. 4 (October 2009): 552–63.

Green, Robert, MD, ed. *Boston Medical and Surgical Journal*, vol. CLXXX (January–June 1919).

Gross, Cary P., and Kent A. Sepkowitz. "The Myth of the Medical Breakthrough: Smallpox, Vaccination, and Jenner Reconsidered." *International Journal of Infectious Diseases*, vol. 3, no. 1 (July–September 1998): 54–60.

Illo, John, trans. "Pasteur and Rabies: An Interview of 1882." *Medical History*, vol. 40 (1996): 373–77. Accessed January 29, 2019.

Jones, Guy B., ed. "Volume One, Number One." *California State Board of Health Weekly Bulletin*, vol. 1 no. 1 (February 18, 1922). Accessed January 29, 2019.

Jones, Marian Moser. "The American Red Cross and Local Response to the 1918 Influenza Pandemic: A Four-City Case Study." *Public Health Reports*, vol. 125, suppl. 3 (2010): 92–104. Accessed January 29, 2019.

Keeling, Arlene. "'Alert to the Necessities of the Emergency': U.S. Nursing During the 1918 Influenza Pandemic." *Public Health Reports*, vol. 125, suppl. 3 (2010): 105–12. Accessed January 29, 2019.

Leonard, Stephen J. "The 1918 Influenza Outbreak: An Unforgettable Legacy." *Denver Post*, April 30, 2009. Accessed January 19, 2017.

Literary Digest. "Back to the Night Cap." Vol. 64, January 10, 1920, 29.

Literary Digest. "The Influenza Plague Spread Terror and Death in the South Seas." Vol 61, May 21, 1919.

Lustig, Alice, and Arnold J. Levine. "One Hundred Years of Virology." *Journal of Virology*, vol. 66, no. 8 (August 1992): 4629–31. Accessed January 29, 2019.

Lynch, Eileen A. "The Flu of 1918." *Pennsylvania Gazette,* vol. 97, no. 2 (November/December 1998). Accessed May 26, 2017.

Ma, Wenjun, Robert F. Kahn, and Juergen A. Richt. "The Pig as a Mixing Vessel for Influenza Viruses: Human and Veterinary Implications." *Journal of Molecular and Genetic Medicine,* vol. 3, no. 1 (January 2009): 158–66.

Mayer, Susan Margaret. "Four Pacific Northwest Reservations and the Influenza Pandemic from 1918 to 1919." Master's thesis, Department of Social Sciences, Emporia State University, April 16, 2012. Accessed January 29, 2019.

McCook, Alison. "Death of a Pathology Center: Shelved." *Nature,* vol. 476 (August 17, 2011): 270–72 Accessed January 29, 2019.

Montagu, Mary Wortley, *Letters of the Right Honourable Lady M--y W--y M--e: Written During her Travels in Europe, Asia and Africa.* Vol. 1 (AIX: Anthony Henricy, 1796). Accessed January 29, 2019.

Morens, David M., and Jeffery K. Taubenberger. "1918 Influenza: The Mother of All Pandemics." *Emerging Infectious Diseases,* vol. 12, no. 1 (January 2006): 15–22.

———. "1918 Influenza, a Puzzle with Missing Pieces." *Emerging Infectious Diseases,* vol. 18, no. 2 (February 2012): 332–35.

Morens, David M., Jeffery K. Taubenberger, and Anthony S. Fauci, "Predominant Role of Bacterial Pneumonia as a Cause of Death in Pandemic Influenza: Implications for Pandemic Influenza Preparedness." *Journal of Infectious Diseases,* vol. 198, no. 7 (October 2008): 962–70.

Mormino, Gary R. "Flu Deadlier Than Bullets." *Tampa Tribune,* May 24, 2009. Accessed February 21, 2018.

Morrisey, Carla R. "The Influenza Epidemic of 1918." *U.S. Navy Medicine,* vol. 77, no. 3 (May–June 1986): 11–19.

Navarro, Julian A. "Influenza in 1918: An Epidemic in Images." *Public Health Reports,* vol. 125, suppl. 3 (2010): 9–14. Accessed May 22, 2018.

New York Times (various)

Philadelphia Inquirer (various)

Pittsburgh Press, October 30, 1918, 1–3. Accessed January 29, 2019.

Popular Science Monthly, vol. 93, no. 6 (December 1918): 65.

Potter, C. W. "A History of Influenza." *Journal of Applied Microbiology,* vol. 91, no. 4 (October 2001): 572–79.

Potter, Polyxeni. "Pale Horse, Pale Rider Done Taken My Lover Away." *Emerging Infectious Diseases,* vol. 19, no. 4 (April 2013): 694–95. Accessed January 30, 2019.

Riedel, Stefan. "Edward Jenner and the History of Smallpox and Vaccination." *Baylor University Medical Center Proceedings,* vol. 18, no. 1 (January 2005): 21–25. Accessed May 11, 2017.

Russell, Francis. "A Journal of the Plague." *Yale Review,* vol. 47 (1958): 219–35.

San Francisco Chronicle (various)

Shope, Richard E. "Influenza: History, Epidemiology, and Speculation." *Public Health Reports,* vol. 73, no. 2 (February 1958): 165–78. Accessed January 29, 2019.

Shreeve, Jamie. "Why Revive a Deadly Flu Virus?" *New York Times Magazine.* January 29, 2006. Accessed January 29, 2019.

Soper, George. "The Influenza Pneumonia Pandemic in the American Army Camps during September and October, 1918." *Science,* vol. 48, no. 1245 (November 8, 1918): 451–56. Accessed January 29, 2019.

South American, vol. 7, no. 1 (January 1919). Accessed January 29, 2019.

Starr, Isaac. "Influenza in 1918: Recollections of the Epidemic in Philadelphia." *Annals of Internal Medicine,* vol. 145, no. 2 (2006). Accessed January 29, 2019.

Summers, Jennifer A. "Pandemic Influenza Outbreak on a Troop Ship—Diary of a Soldier in 1918." *Emerging Infectious Diseases,* vol. 18, no. 11 (November 2012): 1900–1903. Accessed January 29, 2019.

Tumpey, Terrence M. et al. "Characterization of the Reconstructed 1918 Spanish Influenza Pandemic Virus." *Science,* vol. 310, no. 5745 (October 2005): 77–80. Accessed May 3, 2016.

Valleron, Alain-Jacques, Anne Cori, Sophie Valtat, Sofia Meurisse, Fabrice Carrat, and Pierre-Yves Boëlle. "Transmissibility and Geographic Spread of the 1889 Influenza Pandemic." *Proceedings of the National Academy of Sciences of the United States of America,* vol. 107, no. 19 (May 11, 2010): 8778–81.

Van Epps, Heather L. "Influenza: Exposing the True Killer." *Journal of Experimental Medicine,* vol. 203, no. 4 (April 17, 2006): 803. Accessed January 29, 2019.

Vaughan, Victor. "The 1922 Influenza Outbreak." *California State Board of Health Weekly Bulletin*, vol. 1, no. 4 (March 11, 1922): 1–2.

Wedeking, Rachel. "A Winding Sheet and a Wooden Box." *U.S. Navy Medicine,* vol 77, no. 3 (May–June 1986): 18–19. Accessed January 29, 2019.

Weekly Messenger (St. Martinville, LA), November 2, 1918.

Wilkes Barre Times. "Yes, Whiskey is Foe of Influenza, Says Dries." September 22, 1918, 13.

ONLINE

Abedon, Stephen. "PhD/Professor Microbiology OSU." Ohio State University. www.mansfield.ohio-state.edu/~sabedon/biol2007.htm. Accessed February 22, 2016.

Argüelles, Juan-Carlos. "The Early Days of the Nobel Prize and the Golden Age of Microbiology." Hektoen International. 2013. hekint.org/2017/02/01/the-early-days-of-the-nobel-prize-and-golden-age-of-microbiology. Accessed February 8, 2019.

BBC. "Louis Pasteur: The Man Who Led the Fight Against Germs." www.bbc.co.uk/history/historic_figures/pasteur_louis.shtml. Accessed January 29, 2019.

British Red Cross. "VAD Casualties During the First World War." vad.redcross.org.uk/~/media/BritishRedCross/Documents/Who%20we%20are/History%20and%20archives/VAD%20casualties%20during%20the%20First%20World%20War.pdf. Accessed January 29, 2019.

Duffy, Jim. "The Blue Death." John Hopkins Public Health. Fall 2004. magazine.jhsph.edu/2004/fall/prologues. Accessed January 29, 2019.

Genetics Home Reference/US National Library of Medicine, "What Is DNA?" ghr.nlm.nih.gov/handbook/basics/dna. Accessed January 29, 2019.

———. "What Is a Gene?" ghr.nlm.nih.gov/handbook/basics/gene. Accessed January 29, 2019.

Harvard Health Publications/Harvard Medical School.

"How the Influenza Virus Infects a Cell." www.health.harvard.edu/flu-resource-center/virus/how-a-virus-infects-a-cell__3.htm. Accessed January 29, 2019.

Harvard University Library. "Robert Koch." ocp.hul.harvard.edu/contagion/koch.html. Accessed October 17, 2016.

Human Genome Project/Oak Ridge National Laboratory. "About the Human Genome Project." web.ornl.gov/sci/techresources/Human_Genome/project/index.shtml. Accessed January 29, 2019.

Korkis, Jim. "World War One Walt." Walt Disney Family Museum. May 30, 2011. www.waltdisney.org/blog/world-war-one-walt. Accessed January 29, 2019.

McKeithen, Ann. "The Plague Book." University of Virginia. historical.hsl.virginia.edu/plague/mckeithen2.cfm. Accessed April 5, 2017.

National Institute of Allergy and Infectious Diseases. "Video: What Was the 1918 Influenza Pandemic?" www.niaid.nih.gov/news-events/1918-influenza-pandemic-video. Accessed October 29, 2017.

News-Press (Fort Myers). "Evelyn Foss Video Memory." www.news-press.com/VideoNetwork/47208898001/Centenarian-recalls-1918-Spanish-Flu. Accessed September 8, 2015.

New Zealand History. "The 1918 Influenza Pandemic." nzhistory.govt.nz/culture/1918-influenza-pandemic/samoa. Accessed February 9, 2019.

Nieman Foundation for Journalism at Harvard. "Nieman Foundation Launches Guide to Covering Pandemic Flu." October 24, 2009. nieman.harvard.edu/news/2009/10/nieman-foundation-launches-guide-to-covering-pandemic-flu. Accessed January 30, 2019.

———. "The Worst Flu Pandemic on Record." nieman.harvard.edu/wp-content/uploads/pod-assets/microsites/NiemanGuideToCoveringPandemicFlu/AHistoryOf Pandemics/TheWorstFluPandemicOnRecord.aspx.html. Accessed January 29, 2019.

Nobel Prize Organization. "Robert Koch." www.nobelprize.org/nobel_prizes/medicine/laureates/1905/koch-bio.html. Accessed January 29, 2019.

NYC Department of Health and Mental Hygiene. "1914–1922: The Health Department Modernizes" and "1923–1930: Fighting Corruption and Expanding Health Services in the Roaring '20s." *Protecting Public Health in New York City: 200 Years of Leadership, 1805–2005*. 25–34. www1.nyc.gov/ assets/doh/downloads/pdf/bicentennial/ historical-booklet.pdf. Accessed February 9, 2019.

Online Archive of California/UCLA. "Collection of Personal Narratives, Manuscripts and Ephemera about the 1918–1919 Influenza Pandemic, 1917–1923." oac. cdlib.org/findaid/ark:/13030/kt2t1nf4s5/ entire_text/?query=Masks%20have%20saved%20 untold%20suffering%20and%20many%20deaths. Accessed January 29, 2019.

PBS/American Experience, "Influenza 1918." Aired January 2, 2018. www.pbs.org/wgbh/american experience/films/influenza. Accessed May 19, 2018.

PBS/NOVA. "1918 Flu." Aired November 21, 2006. www. pbs.org/wgbh/nova/body/1918-flu.html. Accessed August 22, 2018.

———. "Reviving the Virus." Science Now. www.pbs. org/wgbh/nova/sciencenow/3318/02-poll-nf.html. Accessed February 8, 2019.

Prud'homme-Généreux, Annie, and Carmen Petrick. "Why Was The 1918 Influenza So Deadly? An Intimate Debate Case." National Center for Case Study Teaching in Science/University at Buffalo, SUNY. sciencecases.lib.buffalo.edu/cs/files/1918_influenza. pdf. Accessed January 30, 2019.

Trails End State Historic Site. "Spanish Influenza: Sheridan County Victims, 1918–1919." www.trailend.co/ spanish-influenza.html. Accessed February 9, 2019.

University of Adelaide. "Letters from Turkey by Mary Wortley Montagu." ebooks.adelaide.edu.au/m/ montagu/mary_wortley/letters/contents.html. Accessed August 7, 2017.

University of California Museum of Paleontology. "Antony van Leeuwenhoek (1632–1723)." www.ucmp. berkeley.edu/history/leeuwenhoek.html. Accessed November 17, 2018.

University of Michigan Center for the History of Medicine. *Influenza Encyclopedia*. www.influenza archive.org. Accessed January 29, 2019.

University of Michigan Medical School. "Victor Vaughan, MD, PhD, 1891–1921." www.med.umich. edu/medschool/dean/past_deans.htm#vaughan. Accessed January 29, 2019.

University of Virginia. "Orders Thought Meete by her Maiestie . . ., 1578." historical.hsl.virginia.edu/ plague/osheim.cfm. Accessed February 28, 2017.

US CDC. "How Flu Spreads." www.cdc.gov/flu/about/ disease/spread.htm. Accessed April 27, 2018.

———. "How the Flu Virus Can Change: 'Drift' and 'Shift.'" www.cdc.gov/flu/about/viruses/change. htm. Accessed April 27, 2018.

———. "Pandemic Influenza Storybook." www.cdc.gov/ publications/panflu/index.html. Accessed April 27, 2018.

US Department of Health & Human Services, Surgeon General. "Rupert Blue (1912–1919)." wayback. archive-it.org/3929/20171201191737/https://www. surgeongeneral.gov/about/previous/bioblue.html. Accessed January 29, 2019.

US National Archives. "The Deadly Virus." www. archives.gov/exhibits/influenza-epidemic/index. html. Accessed November 18, 2018.

US Navy. "Influenza of 1918 (Spanish Flu) and the US Navy." www.history.navy.mil/research/library/ online-reading-room/title-list-alphabetically/i/ influenza/influenza-of-1918-spanish-flu-and-the-us-navy.html. Accessed January 30, 2019.

———. "The Pandemic of Influenza in 1918–1919." www. history.navy.mil/content/history/nhhc/ research/library/online-reading-room/title-list-alphabetically/i/influenza/the-pandemic-of-influ enza-in-1918-1919.html. Accessed January 30, 2019.

———. "A Winding Sheet and a Wooden Box" (Josie Mabel Brown interview). www.history.navy.mil/ content/history/nhhc/research/library/online-reading-room/title-list-alphabetically/i/influenza/ a-winding-sheet-and-a-wooden-box.html. Accessed January 29, 2019.

Youngdahl, Karie. "Spanish Influenza Pandemic and Vaccines." College of Physicians of Philadelphia. December 5, 2011. www.historyofvaccines.org/ content/blog/spanish-influenza-pandemic-and-vaccines. Accessed January 29, 2019.

AUDIO

Hardy, Charles, III, producer. "I Remember When: What Became of the Influenza Pandemic of 1918 in Philadelphia." *Talking History*. Albany, NY: State University of New York, March 24, 2005. www. albany.edu/talkinghistory/ind/hardy-remember-when-influenza-epidemic.mp3. Accessed January 29, 2019.